## Mo

"*Gospel Discipleship* is a wonderful resource for the journey to growing into the image of Christ. The author brings a fresh perspective and even a new language to the ancient practice of discipleship. Readers are able to learn more about themselves and gain a new vantage into how those around them best grow as disciples. Are you a Markan, a Matthean, a Lukan, or a Johannine? Take the survey included in the book and find out!"

—Ken Willard, Professional Certified Coach; Director of Discipleship, Leadership, and Congregational Vitality, West Virginia Conference, UMC; author, *Stride*

"*Gospel Discipleship* is a rare book. Michelle Morris takes years of experience and research and gives pastors and church leaders a clear, accessible approach to discipleship in the local church. She recognizes that there is no cookie-cutter approach to leading people deeper with Christ and gives four scriptural pathways that are truly good news for all people. Use this to do our most important work, making disciples."

—Jacob Armstrong, senior pastor, Providence Church, Mt. Juliet, TN

"I've grown as a disciple by participating in *Gospel Discipleship*. I learned about the characteristics of the types: Markan, Lukan, Matthean, and Johannine. I scored almost evenly across all four types. This assessment allowed me to focus on my strengths as a disciple. One of my strengths as a Lukan disciple is building relationships around my table or over food or coffee or tea. As such, leaning into my strengths gave me confidence to meet with people to share the vision for developing a new worshipping community. In addition, I was able to provide them opportunities to learn about their own discipleship type as we sought to reach new people in our community."

—Andreá Cummings, campus pastor, St. Luke, A Campus of Pulaski Heights UMC, Little Rock, AR

Congregation Guide
ISBN 9781501899072

Participant Guide
ISBN 9781501899058

## Streaming Videos

ISBN
9781791008260

ISBN
9781791008277

ISBN
9781791008284

ISBN
9781791008291

ISBN
9781791008307

ISBN
9781791008314

Gospel Discipleship Assessment
www.ministrymatters.com/gospeldiscipleship

MICHELLE J. MORRIS

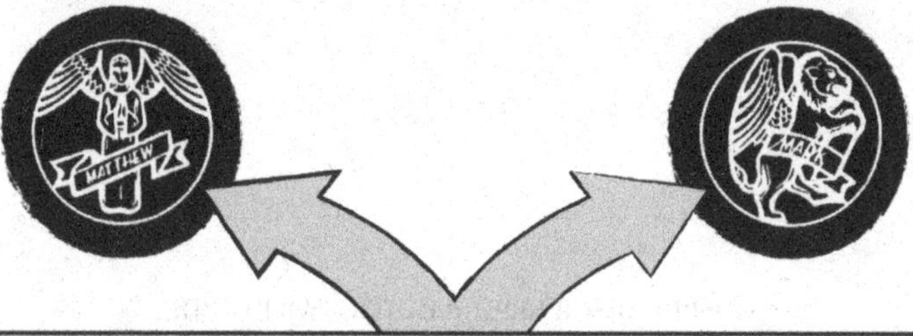

# GOSPEL DISCIPLESHIP

## 4 Pathways for Christian Disciples

PARTICIPANT GUIDE

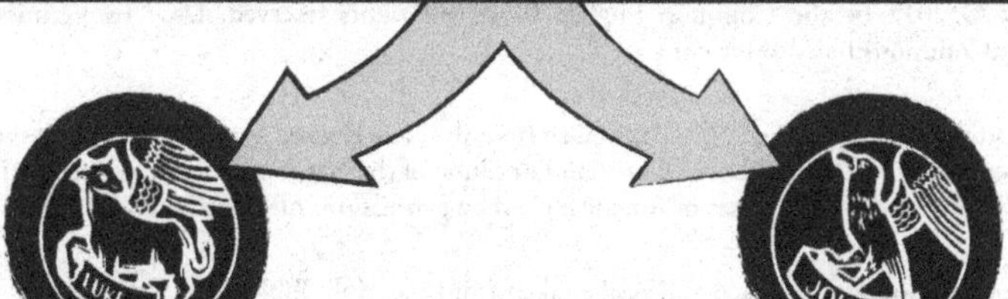

Nashville

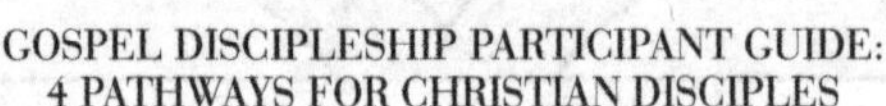

GOSPEL DISCIPLESHIP PARTICIPANT GUIDE:
4 PATHWAYS FOR CHRISTIAN DISCIPLES



ISBN: 978-1-5018-9905-8



20 21 22 23 24 25 26 27 28 29—10 9 8 7 6 5 4 3 2 1
MANUFACTURED IN THE UNITED STATES OF AMERICA

# CONTENTS

# ACKNOWLEDGMENTS

So many people have had a hand in the creation of this work. I would love to name them all, but that would be a book in itself. Instead, the ones named here are representative of all the help I received along the way.

I am first and foremost thankful for my family, who has listened to me ramble on about this idea for nearly a year now. My husband Travis and son Soren also helped test the test, and my mother Harriett took a hundred phone calls as I processed results. They all encouraged me to keep moving forward.

This work would not exist without the wonderful people at Abingdon Press. I am thankful for those who directly guided me, but I am also aware there are many more behind the scenes who brought this work to the light of day. I must mention Paul Franklyn, however, who saw merit in this project, and who gracefully edited it into a much stronger work. I will always be grateful for his insight.

I was sent on this journey as a result of my work in the Center for Vitality in the Arkansas Conference of the United Methodist Church. My director, Rev. Dede Roberts, not only charged me with working with churches on intentional discipleship systems, but also trusted me enough to let me envision possibilities. Her direction came from Bishop Gary Mueller, who also pushed me to seek a scalable way to talk discipleship with the whole conference, even as I insisted that discipleship had to be highly contextual. His challenge directly gave rise to this resource that is both highly contextual and easily scaled to apply to anyone. Thank you for the inspiration, Bishop.

I am grateful for the people who have shaped me along and before this journey: for Dr. Jaime Clark-Soles, who nurtured me into the Bible scholar I have become, and for Rev. David Moseley, who profoundly shaped me as a pastor. He and his wife, Carol, also encouraged me to seek publication for *Gospel Discipleship*, and I am always so profoundly appreciative of their care for and confidence in me.

All along the way, I leaned on a group of people that I routinely call the best ordination class ever. They helped with word count accountability, encouraged me to hit my deadlines, and above all walked with me through a profoundly stressful year, and I will never be able to fully repay them for all they have done for me: Revs. Paul Atkins (who also appears in the video), Chase Green, Andrew Kjorlaug, Jacob Lynn, Sam Meadors, and Daniel Thueson. (Rev. Judy Rudd, who is not in my ordination class, also helped keep me on track.) You are my brothers and sisters, and I love you all dearly.

Some groups of people were very early testers as individuals (early churches will be mentioned in the congregation guide). One such group was my Summer Course of Study students: Sharon Cochran, Gabriel Dominguez, Stan Gonzalez, Terre McGill, Susan Smith, Ross Talbert, Amy Tecumseh, and John Thomas. Another important early group included members of the Arkansas Conference staff: Rev. Jim Polk, Rebecca Davis, Amy Ezell, Caleb Hennington, Day Davis, Jacob Turner, Nancy Meredith, Michelle Moore, Mary Lewis Dassinger, Vicki Brewer, and Cathy

Hall. Cathy was deeply instrumental in the development of this work, championing it and encouraging me when I didn't have the energy. She is also fantastic as one of my Lukans in the video series, reminding all of us that we are more alike than we are different. I am also grateful to other staff who supported this work in administrative ways: Todd Burris, Melissa Sanders, Mona Williams, Wendy Brunson-Daniels, and Palmer Lee. And of course, I have to give deep thanks to Christina Choh, our conference videographer, without whom the videos simply would not exist. She is a conscientious, careful, and creative collaborator, and I am so blessed to have been able to work with her.

And speaking of the videos, I must thank those who agreed to participate, to share their types and their discipleship with the world, so to speak. To Andreá Cummings, the "star" of the show, I could not have asked for a better representative of a four-typer. Andreá not only gave more time to this than anyone, ready to be a professional at any moment, she was also a blast to work with. I am thankful also for Bryan Ayres, Rev. Trinette Barnes, Samantha Black, and Shelley McCarty who all gave freely of their time and energy, and illustrated each type so well you proved my point!

Finally, there are two others who appeared in the video, and who also show up throughout both of these books. They were both so instrumental in this process that I am certain it would not be before you as it is without them. They both invited me in to test their churches, read pieces of the books along the way, held me accountable to deadlines and word counts, and shared their own insights into their respective types. They also both immediately understood this whole system with minimal initial instruction, and then became fantastic sounding boards as more of it unfolded. More than that, though, they are two of my closest friends on the planet. To Rev. Doug Phillips, I am grateful. I am grateful for your intellect and your talent. I am grateful for your willingness to both pull me from the ledge, and to push me to leap. I am grateful that you knew which one I needed even when I didn't. I will never be able to express how impressed I am with you. You navigate life and ministry with such energy as to constantly inspire me. And to Rev. James Kjorlaug, my co-conspirator of *Gospel Discipleship*, you are my Super Markan. You are my template for all things creative and unbound, for someone so passionately driven by and connected to the Spirit as to set me at awe with you regularly. I am so grateful you were willing to share yourself and your art (prophesytothebones.org) through this project. But more than that, I am grateful that you share your friendship with me. This book and my life would not be the same without you. There is no one else I would trust more with these words and ideas than you. Forever, for always, thank you.

# INTRODUCTION

Travis was headed to meet his dad at his dad's fishing cabin on the White River. Travis had been there a few times, so he knew roughly where he was headed. He also had as much of an address as one can have for a backwoods cabin on a river, which is to say he had the address of the convenience store a few miles from the cabin. The difference in this trip from others he had made, though, was that he was coming from the northeast instead of the southwest. The approach would be totally different for him this time.

Well, that's why we have GPS applications on our phones, right? Travis followed the turn-by-turn instructions, which worked fine until he came to the Clarendon Bridge, which was closed. So, he hit the detour option on his app, and the app redirected him around the block and back to the Clarendon Bridge. He tried again. Back to the bridge. The app steadfastly refused to believe there was any way to get where he was going other than by crossing that bridge.

Travis sat there and argued with his phone. After he regained his senses, though, he remembered he had other apps to choose from. Some of those apps often do a better job of taking into account changes in traffic patterns, including bridge closures. He switched apps, and this time he was redirected in a helpful way.

He made it to the cabin and spent a restful weekend catching and eating catfish and crappie with his dad, just like he hoped.

Perhaps something like this has happened to you. Most of us rely heavily on our electronic devices to get us where we need to be. Most of the time, that plan works well. However, those devices don't always take into account who we are and how we like to drive, and they don't know our histories and our desires to go a little out of the way to buy a cinnamon roll from that bakery we love or to detour and see the house where our grandma grew up. The GPS also doesn't know we need to stop and refuel, unless we tell it so. The GPS knows the shortest (or fastest) way to get there, and does not consider who we are and how we love to travel. It also doesn't always take into account bridges that are out.

This analogy for reaching the fishing cabin applies to how any faith community approaches discipleship, usually without accounting for the challenges and possibilities that are present in the journey now.

1. **We have a destination in mind, roughly.** We know the goal is to grow closer to Jesus, to become the people Jesus calls us to be, and to bring other people along on that journey as well. But ask someone how to get there. Go ahead, ask. It's difficult to explain it in a meaningful way, even if the guide has been in church his or her whole life. We know the destination, yet most churches get lost along the way.

2. **We are now coming from a new direction.** Virtually everyone agrees the twenty-first century looks nothing like the middle of the twentieth century or even the 1990s. Yet most churches still insist on looking like

the prior century. If we behave as though Christendom reigns supreme, as it might have been when everyone went to church and was diligently working on their walk with Jesus (though that idealization was never actually accurate), then we would not need to be intentional about our discipleship, and we would especially not need to be able to explain to others how to become disciples. But the world is coming toward Jesus from a new direction, if seekers are coming toward Jesus at all. If we don't get better at explaining how and why people make the journey, then people are going to choose a different path. Indeed, to take the analogy deeper, Travis could have stopped in Clarendon or somewhere nearby and had his fill of catfish. He knew the main reason to go to the cabin was to spend time with his dad. However, in the faith community we are expecting people to make that trip from a new direction while going to see a relative stranger. So, we need to make this journey clear and help people understand why it is worthwhile to make that trip.

3. **The bridge is out, but we are having trouble adjusting.** Maybe you are part of a faith community who has a clear idea about how to get to Jesus. But you are on the other side of the river already. How are people supposed to get to you and to Jesus if the bridge is out, and that is the only way you know to direct them? Sometimes we are so convinced about our personal pathway for discipleship that we don't notice someone else's conception of how to get there. So even when a particular set of directions isn't working and the community is not growing in faith, we still insist people take the path over the bridge that is out. People drown that way. Or give up and never try crossing the river.

4. **There are many ways of getting to the same place.** You probably have your go-to app for directions. Perhaps you just use the app that came preloaded on your phone. If you put in a destination, many of these apps will agree on the path, but they may also give you multiple options for getting there. Maybe you choose one option because you know that path is more scenic than the other, even if it takes longer. Or maybe one will take you by the grocery store and you want to stop and get something for dinner on the way home. The church needs to recognize that even when we all have the same destination in mind, we need and want many different ways of getting there, because we are many different people.

## A New App for Discipleship

*Gospel Discipleship* offers a new app, with familiar reliance on scriptural coordinates for people who follow Jesus. In this case, *app* stands for *approach* rather than *application*. This new approach uses an ancient map, the four Gospels, with a new look at the geography and terrain.

Each Gospel was written to a different community. While each one tells the same story (roughly), each one has a distinct way of getting to the destination, which is bringing people to a life lived for Christ. Each one takes particular detours on that journey in order to reach the people who could be on this path.

The ancient councils who gathered together to decide which accounts of Jesus would make it into our scriptures recognized that different people resonated with different stories, and so rather than putting one Gospel into the canon, they made sure there were four perspectives. These four perspectives provide four distinct pathways for following Christ. Each one appeals to a different group, and so collectively they can call the world to Jesus, especially as the four can be blended to form hybrid paths.

When you find yourself lost, you need someone to give you directions. We are lost in the weeds of discipleship, so it is time for new directions. That is what this guide aims to do. Many of us have taken tests such as the Myers-Briggs Type Indicator, Gallup Strengths, or the Enneagram. The results help us to better understand who we are and how we work best with the people around us. Self-awareness is a powerful tool. Many leaders and churches have used these tools to better understand how to serve together. However, ultimately these are secular models that have had to be adapted to church. They also do not include any component that reflects on how your spiritual life grows with such understanding.

Through *Gospel Discipleship*, you will take a similar test that reveals the kind of disciple you are, again based on the four Gospels. Markans are inspired by the Holy Spirit. Mattheans are action driven. Lukans are focused on relationships. Johannines are nurtured by a mentor-apprentice structure. Once you understand what kind of disciple you are, there is a clear pathway for you to walk to grow in your faith. The path provided is a template frame for that journey. But you will customize it to account for who you are, where your starting point is, and how you need to travel. Gospel-driven discipleship is like having a GPS that points you in the right direction in your faith journey, but allows you to decide when and where you need to stop along the way to enjoy the journey.

In this world where each person customizes life down to the television shows they watch and the music they listen to, we cannot assume that one-size-fits-all discipleship is going to work. In fact, the evidence shows that it has never worked. It is useful to study discipleship as a collective whole, but we can do a better job of understanding the kinds of people who make up that whole. We need to value the gifts and perspectives that seekers and believers bring to the table. *Gospel Discipleship* will help us do that personally and as a community. To begin our journey, just as you would begin a trip to the Grand Canyon, you need to share the relevant information that will point the way. So your next step in this voyage is to share who you are so you can learn how to get to Jesus. For that, we turn to the Gospel Discipleship Type Assessment.

# GOSPEL DISCIPLESHIP TYPE ASSESSMENT

With each of the questions below, choose the ONE answer that you think BEST answers the question FOR YOU. You will most likely agree that more than one, perhaps even all, of the options are true, but choose the one that you think is the best response in your own opinion. The only wrong choice is a choice that does not reflect what you think.

1. Which of these words best describes discipleship to you?

   a. Empowering
   b. Doing
   c. Loving
   d. Learning

2. Which feels most like discipleship to you?
   a. Initiating a new ministry for Jesus that uses my specific gifts and graces
   b. Serving those who are hungry or thirsty
   c. Sitting with someone who is going through a hard time
   d. Learning about the Bible from a great teacher

3. What could best help you understand your faith and how to live it?

    a. A spiritual gifts test and a conversation with someone who can help me discern the results
    b. A basic inquiry class on the vows of membership at your church
    c. A small-group discussion
    d. Meeting with a trusted leader or pastor to talk about purpose (e.g., God's will)

4. What is the best witness to your personal faith?

    a. Living an authentic, faithful life
    b. Doing mission work so people see Jesus in my actions
    c. Spending time paying attention to other people and loving them
    d. Leading through Christ's example

5. Who would you most want to trade places with in the Bible?

    a. One of the disciples when the Holy Spirit shows up on Pentecost (Acts 2)
    b. The Good Samaritan who rescues the traveler assaulted on the side of the road (Luke 10)
    c. One of the people walking on the road to Emmaus with Jesus (Luke 24)
    d. The woman at the well who gets to talk one-on-one with Jesus (John 4)

6. What works best to help you grow in your faith?

    a. Having the freedom to figure out my own path
    b. A defined list of things to work on

c. Collaborating with friends on how to grow

d. Receiving direction from a trusted mentor

7. What is the biggest strength of your particular church?

a. We make space for all kinds of people

b. We have incredible programs and outreach

c. We have wonderful fellowship with each other

d. We offer solid and useful teaching on the Bible

8. What would you like people to say about your particular church?

a. People figure out their life's purpose here

b. People here are the hands and feet of Christ

c. We do life together well

d. Each person matters to us

9. What adjective best describes you?

a. Creative

b. Hardworking

c. Caring

d. Knowledgeable

10. Which word bests describes ideal leaders in a church?

a. Innovators

b. Organizers

c. Companions

d. Mentors

11. Which phrase best describes your ideal pastor?

    a. Encourages and empowers the people
    b. Casts a compelling vision that gets us moving
    c. Walks alongside us through life
    d. Excellent teacher and preacher

12. What is the best way to make a disciple?

    a. Cultivate personal gifts to live fully into the person God calls them to be
    b. Engage in mission and worship together
    c. Build a meaningful relationship that encourages growth through sharing faith with each other
    d. Teach the biblical principles of discipleship (e.g., studying the parables or Sermon on the Mount)

13. What would be a significant faith crisis for you?

    a. If I felt like the Spirit had left me or my church
    b. If I felt like my church wasn't doing anything to change lives
    c. If my Sunday school class or small group got in a fight and dissolved
    d. If my pastor or mentor had a significant moral failure

14. What do you think the purpose of the church is in the twenty-first century?

    a. Helping people recognize and cultivate the gifts God has given them
    b. Making a difference in our community in the name of Jesus

c. Providing space for people to develop authentic, loving relationships with Christ and each other
d. Teaching people how to live like Jesus

15. Which phrase best describes who faithful people of God are?

a. People who know who they are and whose they are
b. People who are transforming the world for Christ
c. People who love God and love neighbor
d. People who follow Jesus

16. When the church is off track…

a. People quit contributing—no one wants to share their gifts with a broken community
b. No one's life is being changed for the better
c. People quit caring about each other
d. The leadership tends to get in trouble

17. To grow in my own discipleship, I need…

a. The chance to start a new ministry that God has laid on my heart
b. To do something—engage in Bible study, help lead in worship, or go on a mission trip—that will move me out of my comfort zone
c. To open my home and my heart to a new small group of people
d. To spend some time learning from the wise people of faith in our congregation

18. The church should…
    a. Pay attention to how the Holy Spirit is moving in its midst
    b. Teach people how to go into the world and make a difference in people's lives
    c. Build a supportive and loving community
    d. Be an example for the rest of the world

19. The church is missing the point when…
    a. It isn't allowing people to use their gifts to serve God
    b. It isn't making a difference in the community
    c. It isn't getting to know its neighbors
    d. Its leadership is failing to lead

20. I have been most frustrated with church when…
    a. I haven't found my place there
    b. We aren't doing anything
    c. People are fighting and gossiping
    d. The pastor isn't helping me grow

21. The kind of pastor who would be best for us…
    a. Nurtures our gifts and empowers us to serve
    b. Is a go-getter who inspires us to work for Jesus
    c. Loves us deeply and is present in our lives
    d. Is a great teacher and preacher of the word

22. The best way to share Jesus with others is to…
    a. Help them understand that they are special to God and God has a purpose for their lives
    b. Show them Jesus by talking the talk and walking the walk
    c. Love them and help them see God in their own lives
    d. Teach them about Jesus in a personal way

Thank you for completing the Gospel Discipleship Assessment. If you take this assessment online at www.MinistryMatters.com/gospeldiscipleship, your score and Gospel Discipleship type can be emailed to you. If your church is taking it together, be sure to email your results to the person compiling totals for your church. For additional resources for this collection, visit www.gospeldiscipleship.net.

To score this assessment on your own, tally up how many times you answered *a*, how many times you answered *b*, how many times you answered *c*, and how many times you answered *d*. Whichever letter you have the most answers for is your primary type. Your second highest score is your secondary type. You may have a tie as well, in which case you share characteristics of both types. The letters each correspond to the following types:

- A = Markan
- B = Matthean
- C = Lukan
- D = Johannine

## How Do You Determine Your Type?

So to start the process of understanding how to intentionally live your discipleship, you need to take it. To do so, take the survey above or go to ministrymatters.com/gospeldiscipleship. Your email address is necessary so that your score can be emailed to you with your Gospel Discipleship type. While answering the survey, it is likely you will desire to choose more than one option on the questions. Each of the alternatives suggest good practices of discipleship! And naturally as learners, we were encouraged by a previous teacher to adopt a particular approach to discipleship. We essentially took the road that was right before us. Nevertheless, please pick the one answer that resonates *most* with *you*! It is important that you live fully into the kind of discipleship God desires, so that you can serve in the ways God needs you. Trying to fit a square peg into a round hole is probably not furthering for the reign of God.

Once you have your results from the survey, return to this book. You are encouraged to read the whole book, but you will probably skim quickly to the descriptions that apply to you. Most people have a primary and a secondary discipleship type. Lean heavily into your primary type, but read up on your secondary type because that will sometimes influence how your primary type plays out. For instance, one of my good friends is Markan (actually, he has no secondary type), and I am Markan Johannine. We were talking one night about whether we like teaching with short notice. Markans, who are driven by the Holy Spirit, tend to move quickly and at the urging of the Spirit. However, the Super Markan (as I call him) said no way would he like to teach with little notice, especially if he did not feel the urging of the Spirit to do it. I, on the other hand, said I only need about five minutes to pull an outline together (assuming it is a topic I have some expertise on, which presumably would be the case if people are asking me to teach) and I am good to go. But my secondary type is Johannine, people who love learning and teaching. So my secondary type has some impact on how my primary type plays out.

You will discover that Markan types are discussed prior to Mattheans, which is not the order those books are found in the Bible. Scholars have developed strong evidence that Mark was written before Matthew, which affects some of the discussion about how Mark's Gospel resonates with Markans.

After you get results from the survey, if they raise some concerns for you, see the last section of the book, which addresses common questions people had through the pilot process.

## But the Point Is...

Most people find that it is fun to learn their discipleship type. When they take the assessment with friends or family, they start to understand more about how they interact and learn from each other. The tool offers useful glimpses into self-awareness as well as an outward orientation toward others who seek to follow Jesus. The primary purpose of this exercise is to help you grow in your discipleship. Such growth happens intentionally. So each chapter on a particular Gospel type provides a reflection on the way discipleship plays out for a Markan, Matthean, Lukan, and Johannine. It closes with an outline of a plan for your discipleship that you can customize. You can also find worksheets at www.gospeldiscipleship.net. We never retire from being disciples of Jesus. To progress in your growth plan, you will return to it again and again. First, return to check in to make sure you are actually progressing, and if not, what adjustments need to be made. Then, return to it so you can refresh it to avoid getting stuck in a rut. You may want to set a reminder in your calendar to return every six months.

You are encouraged periodically to retake the assessment. This applies if you experience a significant spiritual encounter that may alter your discipleship type. Other significant changes in your life can also affect your discipleship. Don't worry if you change: this is the purpose of intentional faith development. Perhaps the Spirit is calling you to a new role in your life. Yet don't worry if you remain the same for a long season. Continue in your steadfast path of discipleship grounded as the person that you are.

By going through this process in community, you can stay accountable to your growth. Therefore, you may want to do this process together as a small group or as an entire church. A *Gospel Discipleship Congregation Guide* is available for group or churchwide use. It goes into more depth about how a particular group or an entire church can live into their dominant discipleship type. It also explores the roles people in nondominant discipleship types contribute in a church that focuses on one thing particularly well.

We all need to stay focused on loving and living for Jesus. In this busy world, it is easy to get distracted from our purpose and our strengths. If this process helps you live more fully into a relationship with Christ, please tell others about it. A website is available with regular blog posts about joys, concerns, and questions that recur on the discipleship pathways: www.gospeldiscipleship.net. Please come visit! You will find ways to share your own story there. Whatever path you choose, may you find yourself closer to Christ and closer to living as the disciple he calls you to be.

# BEGIN WITH THE END

The four paths of discipleship become apparent by looking intently at the four distinct final words spoken by Jesus in each of the Gospels.

In this overview chapter, let's imagine a drone with a camera that is hovering high above a wooded forest. On the ground we can see only the path we are on. But from a high perspective we can see four pathways moving through the forest. The following summary of each discipleship type will orient us to better understanding each other in the midst of forming an intentional faith. The subsequent chapters of this book make a deep dive into the characteristics of each of the discipleship types.

## Mark's Gospel

Some people are excited by the last words of Jesus in Mark's Gospel, and some people think these words are weird. These reactions are a clue that the earliest biographers of Jesus engaged in four distinct ways of living out that discipleship. Those of us who are Markans get excited about the unbound possibilities open in a life committed to holy empowerment.

When we look more closely at the characteristics of Mark's Gospel, we will discuss the fact that there are two different endings to this Gospel. See a good study Bible that makes this point.

For now, we focus on the ending that is before us. Earlier, the women ran away and refused to tell anyone about their encounter in the tomb. Then, in what might be called spiritual whiplash, disciples are grabbing up snakes and drinking poison and healing people! We go from being scared people who run away at the sight of a ghost, to people who are fighting with demons!

This ending to the Gospel speaks of disciples who are EMPOWERED! They are engaged in world transforming work right now! Let's look just at the actions they can now take: go, proclaim, save, condemn,[1] throw out demons, speak new languages, pick up snakes, drink poison, heal the sick. Some of the things on that list are probably exciting to us. Some of them may make us skeptical. Some seem just downright crazy.

Some Christian communities to this day take these words very literally, sometimes to miraculous effects and sometimes to disastrous effects. While grabbing up poisonous snakes to demonstrate God's power is a reliable way to die, the ending to the Gospel does advocate and inspire boundary-pushing thinking. We too often put unnecessary limits on God. Though the Gospel does not mention it directly, we know that the Holy Spirit was sent to empower us for this ministry work. It is no coincidence after the ascension that specific actions performed in Jesus's name are now credited to the Holy Spirit. Jesus ascended, so then we are gifted. We are gifted to do miraculous things. We will do these things in his name, but we will do them because the Holy Spirit has empowered us to bend the world's expectations, to do miracles, and to restore the world. We will be equipped as needed, as the

1. To be precise, "save" and "condemn" are passive constructions, which implies that someone other than the disciples are doing the saving and condemning (i.e., God), but the response to these disciples does result in those actions.

Spirit directs and to the ends God wishes to achieve. So Markan disciples are gifted, and recognize that anyone who seeks to follow Jesus is also gifted, and that together we do transformative work. We do it not by our power but because we are given power from the Spirit. Markan disciples are people inspired by the Holy Spirit and acting on their gifts.

## Matthew's Gospel

These may be the most famous of Jesus's final words spoken in any of the Gospels. This passage is typically referred to as the Great Commission, because Jesus gives his followers such direct instructions about what they are supposed to do in his absence. What they are supposed *to do* is key. These instructions are action verbs for followers to take on Jesus's behalf. Go. Make disciples. Baptize. Teach. Then, Jesus promises a verb of being in answer to all of this doing: "I myself will be with you every day." All that doing results in the people we will be, the people who are with Jesus.

This verse reads as a concise checklist of discipleship. If you want to know how to *be* a disciple of Jesus, then *do* these things. Go. Make disciples. Baptize. Teach. Each verb is both simple and profound, achievable and a lifelong commitment that will never be finished. They are understandable instructions, but instructions without clear definition or limits. Still, they are things we can work with. Actions we can take. Let's look more in depth at each of them and see what they show us about being a disciple.

**Go.** Go on, get moving! Christianity is a faith on the move, a faith that is reaching out to more and more people (all nations in just a few more words in the verse). It is not a faith that huddles in houses, afraid of other people and worried about how new folks might challenge and change us. Instead, Christianity is *meant* to engage in ways that not only challenge but that also change—transform—others as they come to fall in love with Jesus and seek to serve him. Also, this mandate has no limits. It does not define our stopping point. We have to go and go and go, into more and more unfamiliar territory. This may be a new physical location that brings you in contact with new neighbors, or it may be an exploration of new practices of faith that deepens your own faith and the faith of others. Regardless, if we fail to go, we fail at the last instruction Jesus gave us. We're better than that. Jesus knows that too, or he wouldn't have entrusted us with the mission in the first place. So go!

**Make disciples.** We know that God is the creator. We also know, though, that God created us in God's own image. God created us to be creative, and here Jesus also commands us to be creative. Here I mean not only in the sense of creating something but also in the sense of doing so in new and inventive ways. However, we weren't called to make whatever we want. We are called by Jesus to make disciples. We need to be open to the creativity of that work. When was the last time you helped make a disciple? Perhaps it is time to try something new. Do what you need to do to participate in making a new disciple, even if that new disciple is you.

**Baptize.** In the midst of this paradigm-shifting reality on the other side of the resurrection, a couple of things continue to matter: ritual and commitment. Baptism, which usually for us takes place in the context of worship, anchors all that we do in a deep tradition, one that holds worship and the rituals of worship at the center of our faith. Jesus recognizes that as Christianity spreads, it will need a ritual means of distinguishing the transformation. In other words, we need to physically represent this new life that is unfolding. Baptism is that specific ritual, but worship creates the frame through which such continual transformation can occur. It helps us stay focused not on ourselves but on God. Baptism also recognizes that such transformation is challenging work, and we need a community to hold us accountable. So, in our checklist of what it means to be a disciple, we worship (and we bring others to worship).

**Teach.** People won't commit (at least long term) to what they don't understand. Also, how can they be transformed over a lifetime if continual growth doesn't occur? To be at the work of making disciples, we must also be at the work of teaching people what a disciple is. This is the work of making the reign of God a reality, one person at a time. Each disciple is continuously learning how to be a follower of Christ. But each needs to teach the ones coming behind us from the lessons we have learned. It is not a specialized call for those who are gifted at teaching. Each is called to teach, and to teach from our own lives and experiences, so that the people in our lives know how to live more and more like Christ.

Matthew's Gospel gives us these instructions, actions to take on behalf of Jesus. Those who resonate with Matthean discipleship will be people who like to take action, people who prefer defined instructions to follow in order to walk with Christ.

## Luke's Gospel

On the way to the end of Luke's Gospel, we skipped past it and traveled in to the Book of Acts. Why? Because we should read Luke and Acts together. Virtually everyone agrees that both books were written by the same person, and Acts is the continuation of the story of Jesus's followers once Jesus has ascended. Jesus still speaks in Acts. So, to look at the last words in the Lukan narrative, we look at Acts. We are also going to zero in on the very last words, which means we are not going to get drawn into the debate about when Jesus is coming back. Jesus is not that concerned about it, as he deflects the question, saying it's not for any of us to know.

Jesus is setting us on a path of discipleship that radiates out in concentric circles. We start in Jerusalem. Then we move out to Judea and Samaria. Then we go to the ends of the earth. We are directed to do God's work in the world. In the whole world. That's right, from here to there and everywhere we can carry God's gospel of love as exemplified in Jesus Christ!

Discipleship in Acts is about discipleship without limits. We read story after story of limits that come crumbling down, whether it is geographic limits, or cultural limits, or spiritual limits. Nothing bars us from sharing the power of Jesus with anyone the Spirit wants that we set our minds to reaching. NOTHING! More than that, though, there is no one we can't reach for Jesus. NO ONE. Everyone matters to Jesus. He is not concerned with where they live, what language they speak, what nationality or ethnicity they are. Go to everyone. Everyone.

We start small. We start with the people we know, our Jerusalem: ourselves, our families. Then we look at the people that seem familiar, our Judea and Samaria: our small group, our church. Then we go wherever God takes us, even the other side of the world and back again, but certainly into the mission field around us. The point for Luke is to "start." Don't hole up in the safety of your birthplace, because you know what will happen if you do?

The Spirit will show up and huff and puff and blow your Lukan house down.

You will not go alone. Not only will God be with you, other people will be too. When we look closely at the characteristics of discipleship in Luke, no one goes out alone. They typically go in pairs. So as intimidating as it can be to leave the familiar, you will take someone familiar with you. Why? Because Lukan disciples are highly relational people. They are people who are called to make new relationships with new people, but they take someone they know with them when they do it. Lukans will transform the world, from neighborhood to neighborhood, one person at a time, as they introduce themselves to others, and introduce those others to Jesus Christ.

## John's Gospel

We zeroed in on the very last words spoken by Jesus in Acts. In John, however, we are going to zoom wide and take in a significant chunk of the scene, including in part Peter's response to Jesus. We will see from this scene some significant aspects of what it means to be a disciple in John's Gospel.

Jesus instructs Peter to feed his sheep and lambs. Feeding means satisfying hunger, and people can be hungry for many things. It may be actual food. In John, however, a highly symbolic Gospel, Jesus has already offered up his own body as bread for the world (see John 7). The hunger runs deeper here. It is also a hunger of the soul to connect with Christ. And then, along with hunger comes thirst. In John 4 we encounter the woman at the well. She was at the well in the middle of the day to get water, and to avoid other people. Sure, she was thirsty for water. But she was also thirsty for community. She was thirsty for relevance. She was thirsty for a life that mattered to someone, anyone. Jesus quenched her thirst, and he did so by coming to her and engaging with her one-on-one, just as he does with Peter here.

After the instruction to feed, Jesus has to tell Peter twice in the space of what was probably just a few seconds to follow him. Peter is still struggling to learn the lesson that Jesus has been trying to teach all his disciples. You might think Jesus wanted to pop Peter in the forehead. But Jesus doesn't. Jesus just focuses Peter. Follow. Follow. That is what you are supposed to do, Peter. Follow.

Peter was given a private moment on the beach with Jesus, a moment that would allow Peter to understand that his earlier failure is fully forgiven. Peter could have breathed deep in that forgiveness, and then used his next breath to say, "What do you want me to do for you now, Jesus?" Instead, Peter used his next breath to ask about that other guy, the one Jesus seems to really love. *What is going to happen to him?* Jesus tells Peter not to worry about that. *Focus on what I want you to do, which is follow me! That should be enough to occupy your time.*

There is something incredibly powerful about the time and attention Jesus gives solely to Peter in this moment. Jesus has met Peter where he is, healed him of old wounds and patterns, and called him to follow in a way that is particular to Peter, and different from the other guy down the beach. Jesus is working one-on-one with Peter to instruct him in the kind of disciple he specifically is called to be. This is the work of a Johannine disciple: to come to the feet of the one who notices Nicodemus, the woman at the well, the woman caught in adultery, Lazarus and Mary and Martha—all the individuals who populate John's Gospel—and learn directly from him. Then, as a disciple who follows Jesus's path, you in turn teach others what you have learned. Johannine disciples mentor others in the faith, one individual at a time.

Now that we understand how each of these Gospels ends, we can understand how we are to begin. We will all be called to follow, but we will be called in distinct ways. Let's turn now to each type of disciple to understand better what these four ways of following Jesus look like.

Episode One

# MARKAN DISCIPLESHIP

*He said to them, "Go into the whole world and proclaim the good news to every creature. Whoever believes and is baptized will be saved, but whoever doesn't believe will be condemned. These signs will be associated with those who believe: they will throw out demons in my name. They will speak in new languages. They will pick up snakes with their hands. If they drink anything poisonous, it will not hurt them. They will place their hands on the sick, and they will get well." (Mark 16:15-18)*

If you are reading this chapter because you are a Markan, welcome to this pathway! If you are reading to learn about Markans, then you are invited into the wild and creative space that Markans occupy in Christianity. Hopefully by the end of this chapter we will all understand the Markan's charisma a little better.

**Markan Discipleship Pathway**

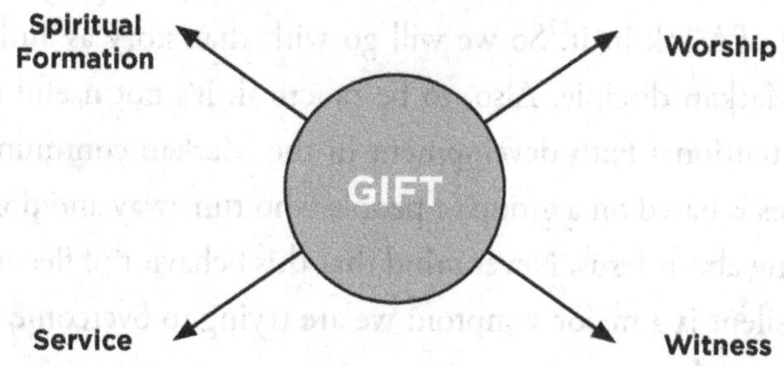

# Representative Characteristics from Mark's Gospel

It's difficult to talk in terms of what is unique to Mark's Gospel because 90 percent of Mark can be found in Matthew or Luke. So how do we determine how Markan disciples are created distinctly from Matthew and Luke? Well, first we can look at how Mark's story of Jesus is structured in unique ways. Matthew and Luke clean Mark up quite a bit. Then, we also look at how its brevity creates a different tone and lifts out different emphases that otherwise get covered up in the longer Gospels. Also, let's remember that the majority of biblical scholars affirm that Mark was the first Gospel written, so even if we are making reference to things that appear in Matthew and Luke, Mark pioneered them.

### *Jesus Seems a Little Unhinged*

It's odd to talk about Mark as the Gospel that emphasizes discipleship in the Holy Spirit. Of all four Gospels, the Spirit appears in Mark the least. Also, to be honest, the Holy Spirit ending appears to be tacked on later. Most scholars acknowledge that the earliest and most reliable examples of Mark we have from antiquity end at 16:8. However, we are shaped by the stories we tell, and the stories we are told. The story we've all been told has the later ending of Mark in it. So we will go with that story as authentic for a Markan disciple. Also, to be practical, it's not useful to say that intentional faith development in the Markan community of disciples is based on a group of people who run away and don't say anything about Jesus. Never mind that this behavior of fleeing and going silent is a major symptom we are trying to overcome in the churches right now.

It is ironic to observe that Mark is our Holy Spirit Gospel. The Spirit of God/Holy Spirit is mentioned in Mark in four places, at 1:8-12; 3:29; 12:36; and 13:11. With the exception of Jesus's baptism, these mentions appear when Jesus is teaching about the Holy Spirit rather than when the Spirit appears. However, consider Jesus's persona in Mark's Gospel. One of the reasons for thinking Mark was written first is that Jesus is a little "rough" in Mark's Gospel. For example, Jesus teaches using a fig tree in Mark, Matthew, and Luke. In Luke's parable, he uses a barren fig and gives the tree a chance to bear fruit (Luke 13:6-9). In Matthew and Mark, Jesus is hungry, comes across a barren fig tree, and curses it. He then uses it to illustrate to his disciples the miraculous things you can do with the power of prayer (Mark 11:12-14 and 20-25; Matthew 21:18-22). In Mark, though, we are specifically told it was not the season for figs (Mark 11:13). But how reasonable is it for Jesus to expect a fig tree to have fruit on it when it is *not the season for figs*?!

It is not reasonable at all. But reason is not necessarily the defining characteristic of the Holy Spirit. The Holy Spirit is free to move at the Spirit's will. The Holy Spirit also bends typical expectations. The Holy Spirit gets us to see things differently, to do things differently, and often deliberately defies typical reasonable expectations to get us to do so. More than in any other Gospel, Jesus behaves like the Spirit does. Father, Son, and Spirit are one in our teaching about the Trinity. There is no reason one can't take on the persona of the other. So Mark's Jesus is canny and unpredictable. So is the Spirit. Markan disciples thrill at living into such boundless creativity, such variety, such unpredictability. Even if it is not the season for figs.

*Power and Authority*

Mark is a spirit-filled Gospel for another reason: a cosmic battle is pitting Jesus against the spirits of demons. Jesus has authority over this spiritual world. How does he have this authority? The legal experts assume that he could command evil spirits because he is aligned with Beelzebub and Satan (3:22). His actions also prompt his family to try to stop him because they presume he is out of his mind (Mark 3:21, a detail left out in the recounting in Matthew and Luke). Jesus, however, reasons that Satan cannot throw out Satan, just as a house cannot be divided against itself. Then, he warns the people that the only unforgiveable insult is an insult against the Holy Spirit (Mark 3:23-29). Jesus clearly has laid claim to the power of the Holy Spirit, and that claim is reinforced by the fact that he can cast out opposing spirits. In fact, Jesus's power is so significant in Mark that even he cannot control it. In Mark 5, when the hemorrhaging woman touches Jesus's clothes, power goes out from him, and he does not know how that happened or who it went to. He has to ask the crowd (5:28-30). Luke recounts the story like Mark does (Luke 8:44-48), but Matthew removes the detail about power flowing out from Jesus and instead tells it as if Jesus takes deliberate action to heal her (Matt 9:19-22). Mark's telling reflects an understanding that God's power is unbounded, even somewhat unmanageable by Jesus.

Mark's Gospel chooses to emphasize miracles such as these over the teachings of Jesus. It's significant that the only stories Matthew and Luke tell about casting out demons come from Mark's Gospel. Neither Matthew nor Luke see a need to add additional stories. Both however, added significant amounts of teaching material. Mark is sparse on the teachings of Jesus. It is clear for the Markan community that the boundary-bending miraculous acts of Jesus are more important than the everyday teachings ordering ordinary life.

Markan disciples are likewise less interested in the practical teachings of Jesus. Instead, they yearn to lean into the miraculous. They seek a faith that doesn't so much help them make it through every day, but that instead changes the everyday into the extraordinary. Markans don't like the same old, same old. They want the radically new and remarkably powerful.

*Building a Mystery*

Often in Mark Jesus tells people not to tell anyone what he did for them. For instance, he orders demons not to tell anyone about him (1:34; also emphasizes his authority over demonic spirits). He tells the man healed from a skin disease in Mark 1:40-44 not to tell anyone. (The man disobeys, as we learn in 1:45.) He also tells his disciples he is the Messiah, and then orders them not to share that with anyone (8:29-30). It seems odd for the founder of a religion to tell his disciples to keep these amazing actions a secret.

On the other hand, Jesus also tells some people to talk about him. For instance, just before he tells demons not to speak because they recognize him, he heals someone else of their demon in front of a crowd of people, who then begin to recognize Jesus's authority themselves (1:25-28). And then, when Jesus heals the Gerasene demoniac, who then wants to travel with Jesus, Jesus refuses him and instead instructs him to return home and tell everyone what God has done for him (5:18-20).

Markan disciples don't really care if Jesus is consistent or not. In the first place, Markans have usually had enough encounters with God's Spirit to know that many things about God cannot be explained. Markan disciples have come to terms with the mystery of God. While Markans do seek encounters with God, Markans do not require the answers for why those encounters happen the way they do.

Additionally, Markans also recognize that context matters. What the Spirit does in one place at one time with one person will rarely be duplicated in another place and another time with another person. The Spirit takes context into account. Markans live into that reality too, and do not assume that what worked in one time and place will work the same in another. In fact, Markans tend to assume that change is always needed. The Spirit adapts, and so should we.

### *Immediately!*

One of the most striking elements of Mark's Gospel is the rapid pace of telling the story about Jesus. It is shorter than any of the other Gospels, but it also hops from moment to moment and barely takes a breath. This rapid movement is underscored by the frequency with which the word "immediately" appears. The Greek word *euthys* shows up seventy times in the New Testament, and over forty of those appearances are in Mark's Gospel. In fact, it is more noticeable when a Markan chapter or passage lacks the word "immediately" than when it has it. Some people even call Mark the "Immediately Gospel."

Markan disciples who respond to the Spirit are people who move at the Spirit's whim. Yes, the Spirit appreciates preparation, usually in the form of regular discernment, prayer, and study. But the Spirit tends to use that foundation to call us forth to move on a moment's notice. Markans learn to be agile in their response.

They look unpredictable and spontaneous, which can have unintended consequences, but the reality is they are waiting to spring into action for the Spirit. And when the Spirit says move, Markans know to move. Immediately!

*Sandwich Stories*

Sandwich stories make reference to the Markan tendency to start a story, then start telling another story, before returning to the first story. It is like bread, meat, bread, and it happens over and over in the Mark's Gospel. Here are a few examples:

- Jesus tells the parable of the sower, then explains the purpose of parables, then explains the parable of the sower (4:1-20).
- Jairus asks Jesus to save his daughter, on the way Jesus heals the hemorrhaging woman, Jesus heals Jairus's daughter (5:21-43).
- Jesus sends out the Twelve, John the Baptist is killed, the Twelve come back (6:7-30).
- Jesus curses the fig tree, Jesus clears out the temple, Jesus and the disciples walk past the fig tree and see it is withered (11:12-21).
- Women are present at the cross, Joseph of Arimathea takes Jesus's body, women are present at the tomb (15:40–16:8).

This nonlinear technique is so frequent in Mark that it is considered a central element to his style. This kind of storytelling resonates with certain people, in our case particularly those who would identify as a Markan disciple. This technique appeals to Markans, who have what could be called "Spiritual ADD."

The reality of leaning into a life with the Spirit is that a Markan disciple's attention holds as long as the Spirit holds it in place. Additionally, as the Spirit is vivacious, Markans grow accustomed to hopping around in focus. It is not that disorienting for a Markan to be deeply focused on something, abandon it for something new for a bit, and then return to a deep focus on the first thing later. This Gospel is written like Markans think and act: never too long in one place on one thing, but willing to return to it to finish up what was started...someday.

## Typical Characteristics of a Markan

Markan disciples are Holy Spirit disciples. As such, their characteristics may seem unpredictable and chaotic to other discipleship types. Well, that's because they are! Highly creative and responsive to the moment, Markans move with the Spirit in surprising ways. But there are a few ways of describing how Markans move and live into their discipleship.

### *Highly Creative*

Markans tend to be the artists, poets, and musicians among us. They are energized by the creation of something new. This includes the creation of new ministries. Markans will think up things that the people of God can do that no one would see coming. They are also the ones who will push the boundaries, primarily because they either don't see boundaries, or because they don't see much purpose in them. They may in fact resent boundaries. How can you hedge the creativity of God? And since we are made in God's image, how can we bind ourselves too? Markans, then, are sometimes the contrary folks like the man at one church who used to hold up a "No Big Words" sign when the pastor started using theological terms that were going over the heads of too many in the congregation. Markans are also likely to be the ones in a meeting who will say the unexpected things that suddenly take momentum in a whole new direction. Markans wholly reject the idea of doing something because we have always done it. Markans know the Spirit is more innovative than that.

*Wildly Inclusive*

Lukans are the highly relational disciples, but Markans actually outdo Lukans on making space for everyone. Markans are not necessarily attached to building deep relationships with people, but they are passionate about making sure there is space at the table for everyone. Why? Because Markans truly believe that everyone has been gifted by God for a special purpose, and if you have walked in the doors of the church, then your purpose may very well be here. You may be the missing piece we need to really catch fire. Markans will even say that any encounter they have outside the church has that potential as well. Because Markans believe everyone has a specific purpose, though, they will only volunteer for the things they know they are called to do. Markans prefer not to step into a role that is not made for them, not because they are lazy but because they know either that role is unnecessary or someone else is called to do it and they should not be so arrogant as to take that person's place. Markans don't like anyone to be ignored, sidelined, or bullied out of their purpose. They may keep the fire in their belly contained in some instances, but keep pushing them to tamp down their passion, and they will eventually erupt.

### *"Short" Attention Spans*

I put "short" in quotes because a Markan can actually hold indefinite attention if the Markan believes the Spirit continues to push in a particular direction. However, as soon as the Spirit shifts, the Markan will want to shift. Immediately. Markans get frustrated that other types do not want to move as quickly as they do (Mattheans can be an exception in some cases). Because Markans turn on a dime, to other types they can appear chaotic and unfocused, but in fact they are hyperfocused, but in multiple directions. One Markan friend, James, coined the phrase *Spiritual ADD*. Markans are easily distracted, and easily bored, but only when Markans either believe we have covered all we need to cover to move, or because Markans believe the Spirit is on to something else. Markans *hate* long, overly conversant meetings. During pilot testing of *Gospel Discipleship,* not only did one Markan make the periodic hilarious remark, but as soon as he detected we were wrapping up, he leaned over and said, "We done?" As soon as he heard yes, he stood up, nodded at the pastor, and walked out. No one flinched, because that is how a Markan relates—immediately.

### *Feel the Presence of God*

Markans know God is active and present in the world today, and they know because they have had an encounter with God. Usually it was profound enough to alter their conception of faith. Of all the types, someone is most likely to suddenly shift to becoming Markan rather than gradually turning into one because of such encounters. Many Markans describe having at least one dramatic, mystical experience of God that may have changed them from the "frozen chosen" to people on fire for God. Because of such encounters, Markans seek the presence of God. Markans are actively looking for God. They hear God as silence, a whisper, or the ground moving beneath their feet. Because Markans are seeking another encounter with God, they know they need to pray, but their prayers will look less like petitions and more like positions: they seek a posture that invites God to show up, rather than going to God with a list of requests. So Markans may pray by painting or doing something else creative because they are seeking to create a space for the Spirit to pour energy into them. For people who tend to be spurred into movement, their prayer space is liable to be remarkably still and profoundly quiet. They will stop everything if there is a chance that God will show up.

### *Open to the Miraculous*

Because Markans know that God is active in the world, they also know that God can change the world. Markans have probably also seen this too. Unlike some who would write off events as coincidence, Markans see the supernatural in the everyday as well as in the extraordinary. That crazy ending of Mark with the poisonous snakes makes Lukans, Mattheans, and Johannines nervous or cynical. Markans have not only seen those things (or their modern equivalent), many of them have done them. Markans get increasingly frustrated with the church because the church too often tries to put God in a box, and Markans know a God totally out of the box, a God who not only bends rules but intentionally breaks them. If there is a sadness to Markans, or a perceived pessimism (which really drives from a place of optimism), it is because Markans have seen what the world could be, and they are deeply frustrated that we make so little progress toward that reality.

*Love Messy*

Markans love a mess because messes happen when the box comes apart. Messes create the margins where the extraordinary can happen. Messes are where people quit trying to put on a mask and instead come forward authentically. Markans know that you can't live fully into the person you are called to be until you are honest with who and where you are. Markans also know that messes accompany creativity. When it comes to worship, they are fine with marginal space—things like people bursting into testimonies or even speaking in tongues. Markans want some variety in worship from time to time, because that creates opportunity to know God in new ways. It may be awkward for the congregation, but that awkwardness forces us to pay attention again. Noticing when things go awry causes us to seek God in that moment, either because we need God's help or because we need to notice what God is doing. Markans want that variety, because Markans know an infinitely different God.

*Markan Spiritual Crisis: Absence or Abuse of the Spirit*

Markans are acutely aware of how difficult it is to feel God at times. There may be a long stretch of time when God feels very distant. However, if a Markan feels as if the Spirit has departed either a Markan's own life or a Markan's church, that disciple is likely to panic. The absence of the Spirit will significantly alter a Markan's life. If a Markan feels the Spirit has left the church in particular, either the Markan will start to "fight like the devil" to right the church and call the Spirit back, or the Markan may leave the church altogether. Additionally, if a Markan detects that someone may be attempting to use the Spirit to manipulate or abuse others, a Markan is liable to react strongly. This is why Markans are particularly equipped to deal with bullies. Markans will see the need for an exorcism of the bullying behavior, which either means the bully needs to change his or her ways, or the bully needs to leave. Markans have a very low tolerance for such evil.

## Living Your Discipleship: Markans

It's wonderful to become aware of what kind of disciple you are. Then we are meant to live it out. For Markans, that means living in the way the Holy Spirit is calling. Depending on how long you have been a disciple and how intentional you've been about progressing in your discipleship practices, you may have experienced different spiritual expressions yet haven't made sense of the intentional purpose. This section connects your type with your purpose.

The suggestions prompt you into pondering what will help you grow. The goal is to be intentional about the means of growth in each of the following discipleship practices: spiritual growth, worship, service, and witness.

*Markan Starting Point: Identify Your Gifts*

Markans want to be intentional in how they grow and serve. That intentionality comes from a desire to follow the directions of the Holy Spirit. Markans also know that the Spirit will gift people to express their discipleship in different and unique ways. Markans also know that the Spirit will sometimes shift gifts. Most people will have a few central gifts that they live out throughout their lives. However, the Spirit may lift one up to the forefront and push one back as there are needs in a person's life and in the community in which that person serves.

For this reason, a critical starting point for Markans is a spiritual gifts test. You may ask, "But I thought that I took a spiritual gifts assessment for this book?" Well, yes and no. This test helped you determine your discipleship type. It did not determine the particular gifts you are called to share in your community. Spiritual gifts include things like teaching, prophecy, speaking in tongues, shepherding, healing, comforting, and more. Markans especially need clarity on their particular gifts, because sharing those gifts is critical to deepening their discipleship.

You can search online for "Spiritual Gifts Test" and come up with a decent assessment. However, you might check out https://www.ministrymatters.com/all/entry/4640/spiritual-gifts-discovering-and-using. In the absence of an assessment, you may seek wise counsel. If you are a Markan in a Markan church, you probably have a fair number of people who have the gift of discernment. Spend time with those wise people, and they can probably advise what your gifts are. Once you know your gifts, that will help you make decisions about how you move through the realms of discipleship. Depending on whether you are a new disciple, a growing disciple, or a seasoned disciple, you will need to adjust your growth in each realm. For example, depending on your previous experience, you may be a beginner in witness but a seasoned pro in intentional spiritual practices. Push yourself from whatever point you start to the next one. This journey is lifelong; we never stop moving forward in the Spirit.

*Realm of Discipleship: Spiritual Growth*

Growth in the Spirit is the purpose of a Markan's life! Markans in particular should emphasize growth in prayer. Remember that prayer for Markans is more about listening than speaking. So for an early disciple, who may know how to bring requests to God but not how to listen, prayer may need to start there and gradually make more space for listening. A seasoned Markan should be able to engage in long stretches of contemplative prayer. The journey in between can lead to different experiments in prayer.

Markans should also read the Bible in community. They would do really well to read in diverse community too. Markans will appreciate hearing from different perspectives. That kind of space creates a rich opportunity for the Spirit to speak through the noise.

Then, each Markan should also look at your own particular gifts. How do those gifts direct you to grow in your connection with the Spirit? Do you have the gift of teaching? Then perhaps you are called not only to grow in your own practice of prayer, but to teach others about it. Do you have the gift of healing? Then perhaps you can learn about healing practices in Christianity, and how those can be nurtured in you and then practiced in community. Take time to reflect not just on typical needs for Markans but spiritual needs that are particular to you.

### *Realm of Discipleship: Worship*

All Christians need to be in worship. Markans, though, seem to be either energized or drained by worship. Much of it has to do with whether they feel the presence of the Spirit or not. Markans will seek worship that has Pentecostal elements to it. Yes, this might be a place in some faith communities where people feel gifted for speaking in tongues. But even in "calmer" Markan spaces, there should be room for creativity. Who brings that creativity? Markans. So if you are a Markan disciple, you need to bring yourself to worship. Early Markan disciples may just want to start with the discipline of being focused enough to attend worship. It is fine if you need to hop around from time to time to different places, times, and styles, but at least make the commitment to worship. As Markans grow in their discipleship, they need to be open to contributing to worship in some way. This could be through offering a testimony, creating a beautiful altar space for a season, or sharing liturgical dance. The most mature of Markans will also learn to take spontaneous worship out into the world. Mature Markans will recognize holy spaces, and will know how to lead others in worship, whether it is within the walls of the church or not.

Again, reflect on your own gifts as well. Do you have a gift of tongues? Then you may cultivate the gift by seeking worship where ecstatic speech is welcome. Do you have a gift for making music? Then make sure you are pushing yourself to express that gift. Join the choir or band if you haven't already. If you have, have you worked up to a solo? Or helped direct the children's program? Push yourself in ways that use and grow your gifts.

*Realm of Discipleship: Service*

The spiritual gifts test that Markans take should be particularly clarifying for them in the realm of service. Especially as Markans grow in their faith journey, they come to understand that the Spirit gifts a community to do the work a community is called to do. They also understand that if you volunteer to serve in a way that you are not called, you can get in the way of the plans. Markans are called to serve in all aspects of the church and community, but their call is very individual both to them and to the time in which they are called. This means that a Markan's call will change as the times change. It is critical that Markans not get boxed in to the kinds of service they do. It takes a little while to discern where you are called, especially in the early days of discipleship. In the first place, a Markan may not feel equipped to do a certain ministry or fill a certain role, even if it tugs at her heart. So she may make a few missteps as she learns more about herself and the community. Give yourself some permission to make that journey, but keep putting yourself forward, especially for the things that your gut or heart says you should do. Markans deep in their discipleship journey should be willing to create new ministries. In fact, the Spirit should be directing you that way. Do not be afraid of crazy ideas. Uncapping the crazy is how the Spirit works. Be brave and step into the vision she has for you.

### *Realm of Discipleship: Witness*

The strength of Markan witness is in the fact that Markans value all people and see all people as gifted by God. It doesn't even matter to them if that person believes in God. Markans know that God is gifting them anyway. Markans, then, can help connect people to their purpose. A Markan early in his journey could practice witness by committing to pay attention to someone. Identify a person and learn more about that person. Find out what ignites that person's passion. Then do something to help that person express that passion, whether that expression is inside or outside the church. Then, as you grow in greater understanding, share with that person how you understand that the passion is a gift from God, and help that person live into giving that gift for God. Each time a Markan concentrates on walking intentionally beside a person, the Markan will get better and better at sharing God with others. Mature Markans, then, should think seriously, in tandem with their growth in worship, if they are called to start a new faith community in a new place for the church.

Additionally, Markans are especially good at reaching people on the margins. Markans see the value in everyone, so they can reach those who are poor, who have chaotic lives, who have tattoos all over their bodies (many Markans will have tattoos anyway, as James shows in the video), artists who think church is too boxed in for their minds and souls. . . . Basically, if the church has either been perceived as unwelcoming, or has actually been unwelcoming, Markans can leave the box and reach the people where they are. And of course, if someone defines themselves as Spiritual but Not Religious (SBNR), Markans know how to support them, because Markans are also SBNRs, yet SBNRs who may also be in a church.

## Your Plan for Living as a Markan Disciple of Jesus

What are your top spiritual gifts?

What will you commit to do to use those gifts to develop your discipleship concerning:

Spiritual growth—

Worship—

Serving—

Witness—

Mark your calendar to return to this commitment six months from now and again one year from now to see how you are doing and if it is time to try something new.

Episode Two

# MATTHEAN DISCIPLESHIP

*Jesus came near and spoke to them, "I've received all authority in heaven and on earth. Therefore, go and make disciples of all nations, baptizing them in the name of the Father and of the Son and of the Holy Spirit, teaching them to obey everything that I've commanded you. Look, I myself will be with you every day until the end of this present age." (Matthew 28:18-20)*

If you tested to be a Matthean disciple, then you are chomping at the bit to learn about yourself so you can get to the task of discipling. If you are interested in Mattheans but aren't one, you are probably wondering what all the hurry is about (though if you are Markan, then you may get it). You are about to learn why Mattheans are anxious to take action. So let's go!

## Matthean Discipleship Pathway

| | Beginning | Intermediate | Seasoned |
|---|---|---|---|
| Spiritual Formation | | | |
| Worship | | | |
| Service | | | |
| Witness | | | |

# Representative Characteristics from Matthew's Gospel

### *The Churchiest of Churchy Books*

Of the four Gospels, Matthew is the only one that mentions the word we translate as "church." The word is *ekklesia*, which is also the root of "ecclesiastical," and appears in Matthew 16:18 and 18:15, 17. It is in Matthew that Jesus renames Simon Peter, and explicitly adds that it is on this rock that Jesus will build *the church* (Matt 16:18). The concern with making sure people know that this church was authorized by God, and then led by Peter, may have been a live concern for the early church. It may also explain why Matthew has more material about Peter than any other Gospel. If the early church envisioned itself as founded by Jesus, but then handed over to Peter, then clearly lining out that process would be important.

In fact, Matthew is also concerned with correcting the behavior of church leadership. Matthew is quick to point out ways the Pharisees are behaving, which are not in line with the actions leaders should be taking. While both Matthew and Luke have a list that could be called "the woes of the Pharisees," Luke lists only six, while Matthew lists eight (found in Matt 23:13-16, 23, 25, 27, and 29). Matthew and Luke likely drew from a common source for this list, but it is interesting that Matthew lists more of them than Luke. Also, Matthew is written after the fall of the temple, when the Pharisees rose to prominence in Judaism. Rather than the priests, the Pharisees would be an applicable comparison to church leaders for Matthew's contemporary audience.

Matthew is also organized similarly to a worship service based on the life of Jesus. The good news about Jesus begins with stories of his birth and it is closed with stories about his death on the cross, resurrection, and ascension into the heavens. In the middle, though, are five sections centered around teaching. The transitions occur as each section ends with these words or something similar: "when Jesus finished these words" (see 7:28; 11:1; 13:53; 19:1; 26:1). This book is organized into a flow that would have resonated (and still does) with people who resonate with "church" and a highly organized, teaching-centered worship service.

Matthean disciples, then, are drawn to church. In addition to the experience, Mattheans are drawn to the structure, the ritual, and the practices. These are behavioral parts of our faith. And those behaviors take place in church. Mattheans are very committed to church. They like being part of an "organization," religious or otherwise, but religious organizations definitely tend to equip them to live a life in action for Jesus.

### *Not One Jot or Tittle*

Mattheans prefer organization, and that also comes from an ability to pay attention to detail. This attention to detail is evident in Matthew 5:18 when Jesus mentions that "neither the smallest letter nor even the smallest stroke of a pen will be erased from the Law until everything there becomes a reality." The King James Version translates this with the idiom "not one jot or tittle" would be erased. Matthew is concerned with the details, and particularly the details of the organized part of faith: the law.

Jesus in Matthew did not come to abolish the law and the prophets, but to fulfill them (5:17). In fact, part of the Sermon on the Mount is not just about affirming the law but applying it. Don't murder? How about don't even carry anger in your heart! It looks like Jesus is teaching us to follow the deeper intent of the law. Jesus is taking time to spell out the implications for his Jewish followers. Where there has been ambiguity or evasion concerning the teachings from Moses, Jesus clarifies what is important.

The attention to the smallest detail and the intent to clarify the plan fits well in a Matthean mindset. Not only does it preserve the tradition of the faith community, it also lays out expectations intentionally. This attention to detail around the law tells Mattheans what they should do, how they should do it, and to some extent why they should do it. Mattheans are people of action. In order to take action, they need direction. This Gospel portrays

Jesus as the new Moses, and it reads like an instruction manual. Matthean disciples are grateful for the instruction.

*"My Yoke Is Easy"*

Matthew is the soundbite Gospel. It is very quotable: do not judge or you will be judged also (7:1); ask and it will be given to you, seek and you will find, knock and the door will be opened to you (7:7); no one can serve two masters (6:24); do not put your Lord your God to the test (4:7); let the dead bury their dead (8:22). Many others could make this list. In a web search of favorite verses from Matthew, one passage consistently made the lists: "Come to me, all you who are struggling hard and carrying heavy loads, and I will give you rest. Put on my yoke, and learn from me. I'm gentle and humble. And you will find rest for yourselves. My yoke is easy to bear, and my burden is light" (11:28-30).

This saying makes two assumptions. First, it assumes that people are struggling hard and carrying heavy loads. Poignantly, this saying precedes another confrontation with the Pharisees when the disciples are caught picking grain on the Sabbath. Two types of work are mentioned in that confrontation: disciples picking grain and Pharisees defending the law. Matthew's Gospel stands often in between those two types of work: physical labor and doing right by our faith.

Mattheans are good at carrying burdens. They may carry emotional, intellectual, and physical burdens. Mattheans are hard workers. They do, however, appreciate when that hard work can be made easier. Working with a purpose like serving Jesus helps ease the weight of whatever work they carry. Mattheans resonate with this verse, so much so they may have it tattooed across their back in the position where a cross would rest if being carried.

Such was the case of a man who tested as a Matthean disciple in the pilot run of this assessment. It is important for Matthean disciples to have clarity about what burdens they are supposed to pick up and what ones they should let lie. The ones Christ calls them to will be light; the ones he doesn't will wear them down to exhaustion. In fact, Mattheans recognize, faster than some other types, that if a burden is too heavy to carry, it may need to be set down. They will raise the question, "If this is too hard to carry, does it really reflect God's will for us?" They may struggle to put it down because they don't want to fail at working for God. Yet they know Christ's burden is light. They aren't afraid of hard work. They are afraid of wasting their time and energy on something that is not called for by God.

*Concentrated Focus on the Teachings of Jesus*

Matthew's last instructions from Jesus to his disciples is to teach. There are more of Jesus's teachings found in Matthew than in any other book in the Bible. The shining example comes in the Sermon on the Mount, followed closely by missionary instructions and the parables.

Both the Sermon on the Mount and the parables teach people how to live. In particular, they teach people how to live as if the kingdom of heaven is real among us. The Sermon on the Mount (Matt 5–7) describes the states that denote who is a good follower of Jesus. The Beatitudes come to mind as an example. But also, as mentioned earlier, the Sermon on the Mount spells out how to live fully into the law.

The missionary instructions (Matt 10) are explicit recommendations for those who would carry Jesus's mission into the world. The difference between Luke and Matthew in recounting these instructions is striking. Where Luke tells the Seventy-Two who are commissioned that they are to go and spend time in houses with people, living with them and healing them *before* sharing about Jesus, Jesus commissions the Twelve to come in the door announcing the kingdom of heaven is at hand, and then to engage in a series of actions that will prove it.

As for the parables (Matt 13), they are illustrations about the kingdom of heaven that primarily use examples from ordinary life. The elements used are often tied to work that took place at the time: soil, the farmer, weeds, treasure, merchant, net. Jesus is teaching how faith integrates into everyday life and affects all that people do.

Mattheans love to be taught, and to some extent they love to teach. However, unlike Johannines who learn for the sake of learning, Mattheans learn for the sake of doing. The teachings of Jesus here resonate with Mattheans because they clearly tell Mattheans how to live. There is purpose to learning what Jesus has to teach, and that purpose is to change our lives and the lives of the people around us through the actions we take to make a better world—a world in which the kingdom of heaven is plainly evident.

## *Jesus Checks All the Boxes*

Matthew builds a case for why people, in particular Jews, should follow Jesus. Matthew is written in a Jewish context. It is written in the time when Jews are looking for a leader. In particular, they are looking for the Messiah, especially since their Temple is gone. What are they supposed to do now?

Matthew says that all they need to do is start following Jesus. He keeps in line with the tradition. His genealogy puts him in the proper line of descent to be the anticipated Messiah. He also is definitely in the family of Abraham, even if he expands the mission to include Gentiles. People can look back and find him all over the Torah (Matthew quotes the Septuagint more than any other Gospel writer). Jesus is the new, and better, Moses. In other words, if you are looking for someone to follow, Jesus checks all the boxes.

Mattheans are followers, but they will only follow leaders who seem to fit the plan. It is important for someone who intends to activate Mattheans to show that they have planned things out, and that they are fitting within the system. Sure, Mattheans are willing to change the system, but it needs to make sense within a plan, and it needs to connect where we have been to where we are going in a discernible way. This is why Mattheans resonate well with intentional discipleship systems, vision statements, and ministry action plans. They like to know where they are going, and how they get from point A to point B. The Gospel spells that out for Jesus. Mattheans now want a leader to spell it out in our context. In the same way, Mattheans are on the path to becoming church leaders. If a designated leader can't do it well, then a Matthean will step up and do it for you.

## Typical Characteristics of a Matthean

Mattheans are the disciples with an active faith. If you need something done, call a Matthean. Actually, you probably won't even need to call them. They are probably already there. Their defining biblical verse might actually be James 2:17: "In the same way, faith is dead when it doesn't result in faithful activity." With that in mind, let's look at what characterizes the actions of these disciples.

### *Just Do It*

Nike's got nothing on Mattheans. Mattheans don't even need someone to tell them to do something in most cases. They are already doing whatever needs to be done, often before anyone has asked. Mattheans see a need and then they fill it. That's not to say they don't appreciate a good plan, though. In fact, Mattheans love plans and planning, and they thrive with a to-do list. To-dos are what they do! Mattheans are the kinetic people of a church. Basic rule of thumb is, if you need something done, call a Matthean.

### *Lead, Follow, or Get Out of the Way*

Mattheans are as likely to lead as they are to follow. First, they love to be the followers of Jesus. They love to listen to and learn from the teachings of Jesus. But they learn not for the esoteric value but so that they know what they need to do for Jesus. Mattheans are hardworking, hands-to-the-plow people. So give them good instructions, and they are happy to follow them. However, Mattheans don't have a lot of patience for disorganization, so if the leadership is not driving toward action or is making things unnecessarily complicated, a Matthean is likely to step in and take the reins. Mattheans who have a clear vision for how things should be done will step into leadership. Mattheans might become aware that their matter-of-fact approach can be off-putting for Lukans in particular. Mattheans are not likely to see that, though, because they just want to get things done. People can either be their greatest asset in that work, or an annoying hindrance. Mattheans want people who are hindering to align with the priorities or get out of the way.

### *Here We Are to Worship*

Mattheans love all the things that go on at church. Mattheans are likely to be the drivers of many church programs. Most dear to Mattheans, though, will be worship, and Mattheans think everyone feels the same way. Mattheans expect full participation in worship. They usually appreciate unison prayers or shared creeds. They expect people to sing the songs, or at least stand and move to the music. Mattheans affirm vows, liturgy, and expect that lay people are contributing significantly to worship. Also in appreciation of to-do lists, Mattheans will appreciate a bulletin or order of worship. If there is not one printed or displayed on a screen, then liturgical patterns should be predictable from week to week, so people know what to do next. Mattheans can be flexible in their order of worship, but they prefer an alert that such things are going to occur, so they are ready to do the right thing.

### *Missionary People*

All the types get something out of missions, but Mattheans in particular thrive in this work. Going out to people in need and doing something to make their lives better—that is where the rubber meets the road for Mattheans. While often these opportunities are short-term or one shot missions, Mattheans that commit to something more transformative do have the capacity and diligence to stick with something over the long haul. Mattheans need to be taught that this type of work is worth it, because the immediate results are not always visible when working to dismantle unjust systems. If Mattheans can't see that things are changing, they are liable to stop the effort because they do not like to work without purpose. Mattheans also tend to take on practically any project that comes their way. For this reason, a mission statement of purpose is necessary. Mattheans need crystal clarity about what sorts of things they should focus on. A clear mission statement and a vision for accomplishing that mission helps keep them focused.

### *The Overvolunteers*

Mattheans need clarity of mission because they will volunteer for practically anything. They will particularly volunteer if no one else steps forward quickly enough. A project or task that has no one lined up creates anxiety for Mattheans, and they are likely to volunteer rather than asking if the project is truly one that reflects the passions and gifts of the people. In other words, Mattheans will keep doing something because it is something to do (or something we have "always" done). They don't like to leave things undone, unlike Markans who will assume if the right person is not stepping forward, then it is definitely time for that thing to die. Because Mattheans will continue to put themselves forward over and over and over, though, they do have a tendency to exhaust themselves. Churches tend to attract Mattheans because they keep things running, but churches really need to love and support Mattheans by only asking them to do things that serve the mission and vision of the church. A church who doesn't have clarity will eventually lose its best workers, simply because the church wore them out.

### *Matthean Spiritual Crisis: We Did Nothing, or We Did Harm*

Mattheans will lose their mind in a place that is not doing anything for others. A church that sits around or gazes at navels will run Mattheans off. Mattheans need to be doing something, and they need to be doing something that is making a difference in the lives of people. Some of these people can be within the church community, but Mattheans need to see that the church is reaching out too. Another thing that will cause deep issues for a Matthean is if they learn that the work they did actually caused harm. Learning that the short-term mission trip they took to the developed world actually caused problems for the people rather than improving their lives will upset Mattheans. The good news is that well trained Mattheans can take time to consider the consequences of the actions they take leading the church into healthier types of work. So a church leader can watch and listen so that the Matthean does not become so disillusioned as to walk away from church altogether.

## Living Your Discipleship: Mattheans

Living their discipleship is what Mattheans do. However, as with any of the types, it is easy enough to lose focus and get off track, or to get so stuck in a behavioral rut that you just keep doing the same things over and over and over again, without really growing in your discipleship. So Mattheans as much as anyone need to stop the hamster wheel from time to time and reflect on what they are doing and whether it is truly helping them grow.

Mattheans do well with checklists and to-dos, and so their discipleship can work in a similar way. In this section, Mattheans are guided to build a discipleship checklist. Again, these are suggestions, and I invite you to fill in the blanks in a way that is meaningful for you and allows you to move closer to Jesus in the process.

*Matthean Starting Point: Chart Your Path*

The need is for a process of building an intentional way of staying on track in your discipleship, and a list of things to do could satisfy that need. What might be more effective, however, and what might allow you to envision deeper discipleship over a longer time, is to create a chart that allows for growth.

Start with categories across the top of the table that define what level of discipleship you find yourself in. You may use levels such as seeker, beginner, intermediate, median, advanced, mature, seasoned, etc. Unless you are brand new to practicing discipleship, try have at least two competence levels.

Then, down the side of the chart, you would put the practices you want to develop. For the purposes of this book, and in the following example, the practices mentioned are the same core practices across the four discipleship types. However, you can use labels more particular to your tradition. For instance, United Methodists could list the vows we take when we join a church: prayers, presence, gifts, service, and witness. Or we could do a threefold pattern around the General Rules from John Wesley: do no harm, do good, attend upon the ordinances of God (which means ways of staying in love with God). Then, once you have those categories defined, you fill in with actions you take for each level. Then you can use this chart to track your progress. To give you a clearer idea of how this works, let's apply this to four realms of discipleship.

| Practice | Seeker | Novice | Competent | Advanced |
|---|---|---|---|---|
| Spiritual Growth | | | | |
| Worship | | | | |
| Service | | | | |
| Witnesss | | | | |

*Realm of Discipleship: Spiritual Growth*

The activities that would fall under the category of spiritual growth would primarily be those actions that focus on your own personal growth. These can include prayer, studying the scriptures, fasting, even healthy living (see Wesley's "works of piety" for example). Mattheans will not lack for things to do. Mattheans need to think about, of all the things they could do, which ones will help them grow toward the next step. So pick a couple of categories, perhaps studying scripture and healthy living, and define what you need to do to push you to the next level in your journey. Maybe it is something like getting up fifteen minutes earlier to read your Bible or making time in the afternoon for thirty minutes of exercise. Perhaps it is more ambitious, such as agreeing to lead a Bible study or working to reduce the number of medications you are on.

Mattheans should keep one discipleship realm on their list, even if they are good at keeping it: Sabbath. This does not mean going to church on Sunday (that comes in the next discipleship realm). No, the practice of intentional rest is a requirement for Mattheans: for a whole day, every week. It will be a rare Matthean who is good at this practice. Still, it is critically important for Mattheans. Mattheans work themselves hard. They need to be as intentional about rest as they are about work. The struggle in itself is proof that Mattheans need to keep Sabbath.

*Realm of Discipleship: Worship*

Wow, worship is where Mattheans will thrive! Mattheans usually love worship. In the first place, it is the high moment of church life together. Mattheans are church people (even if church takes on many appearances to Mattheans). Mattheans also love corporate activity.

Yet Mattheans need to make sure they keep moving forward in the discipline of worship. This movement can take several trails. Perhaps it is moving from not singing the songs or hymns to singing (though usually Mattheans sing). Perhaps it is volunteering in a new way, including serving as an usher or greeter. Or for some with gifts it is agreeing to train as a liturgist or joining the choir. Or if you are a seasoned Matthean, maybe it is time to train to be a lay speaker who can occasionally deliver a message in worship. The growth Mattheans need from worship is through sharing their gifts. Sometimes this is accomplished by increasing what they give when the offering plate passes by; an offering is active growth as well. But sometimes it is an increase in how they share themselves with others and God in a worship space. Define how you need to grow for now, and how you need to grow in the near future, and add that to your worship-related category.

*Realm of Discipleship: Service*

Some may wonder if Mattheans coined the phrase *worship service*. Mattheans love to serve. They believe that their faith is best expressed in action. Usually, then, Mattheans are serving in some way that expresses their faith. The challenge is usually not finding a way to serve. Rather it is either finding a new way to serve or limiting how they serve so they do not burn out. So Mattheans can use their chart to help them clarify their purpose. For the realm of service, a Matthean lists all the things they already do, and then assesses which ones are still allowing growth. If a Matthean has grown past something, but it is still an important ministry, possibly the Matthean either needs to move into a more significant role of leadership, or if they are already leading, then possibly the thing to do is train someone else to take over leadership, and then step back to move onto something new. Use this process not only to grow in your discipleship but also to set some healthy boundaries around service.

Mattheans sometimes need to make adjustments in the realm of service or outreach. Mattheans prefer short-term or one-off missions. This comes from the expectation of immediate results. Results make Mattheans feel as if they did some real good. In some cases, however, such short-lived acts actually cause problems for the recipients, or perpetuate systems of oppression. If more Mattheans understood that, they would be horrified, since Mattheans deeply desire to avoid harm. Mattheans, then, can also grow in their discipleship of service by looking at dismantling oppressive systems. It is harder work, has less immediate payoff, but ultimately changes more lives.

*Realm of Discipleship: Witness*

Sharing the faith or witnessing is often a realm where Mattheans struggle, which is a struggle for the rest of us too! Mattheans struggle with verbal witness because many live by the principle that you speak your faith by the actions you take. People will see that you are doing good, and that is your gospel witness. That principle seems to work effectively in a culture where nearly everyone doing good is presumed a faithful Christian. Now, though, Christians are perceived to be as likely as anyone to do good or harm. So merely doing all the good you can, albeit missionally, is not as effective at this time for producing more Jesus followers.

The final words of Jesus in the Gospel—the Great Commission—show that Mattheans ought to be good evangelists. Put it on your chart. Then define little steps to help you grow in this space. Start by practicing faith sharing in church. Some call this testimony. Then work at getting more comfortable in the world sharing your faith. Perhaps offer to pray for or with your server at a restaurant. Or ask to pray for your grocery checker. Mattheans who are practiced in opening up about their faith will typically be the ones who can strike up these kinds of conversations with strangers. They do it because that is what you do. And let's not forget a basic action of witness is the act of inviting. Mattheans are well suited to actually invite people to church, and to go pick them up and then take them out for lunch. Whatever step you need next to share the good news of Jesus Christ with people, define that action and start acting on it.

# Your Plan for Living as a Matthean Disciple of Jesus

See the sample table on page 54. List at least two categories of stages for your discipleship (e.g., beginning, intermediate, advanced):

List the types of practices you need for your discipleship:

Brainstorm possible actions under each practice and stage.

Draw your chart and start checking boxes. Update and revise the chart as you complete a column.

Episode Three

# LUKAN DISCIPLESHIP

*He said to them, "This is what is written: the Christ will suffer and rise from the dead on the third day, and a change of heart and life for the forgiveness of sins must be preached in his name to all nations, beginning from Jerusalem. You are witnesses of these things. Look, I'm sending to you what my Father promised, but you are to stay in the city until you have been furnished with heavenly power."*

*As a result, those who had gathered together asked Jesus, "Lord, are you going to restore the kingdom to Israel now?"*

*Jesus replied, "It isn't for you to know the times or seasons that the Father has set by his own authority. Rather, you will receive power when the Holy Spirit has come upon you, and you will be my witnesses in Jerusalem, in all Judea and Samaria, and to the end of the earth."*
*(Luke 24:46-49; Acts 1:6-8)*

So you are a Lukan. You love everyone. You want to welcome everyone. Also, you want to be welcomed. To live into your call of love, it is important to understand what it means to love, and how loving others has its great joys and its challenges as well. Hopefully this section will give you the description you need to live fully into a life of abundant love for others and for God.

## Lukan Intentional Discipleship

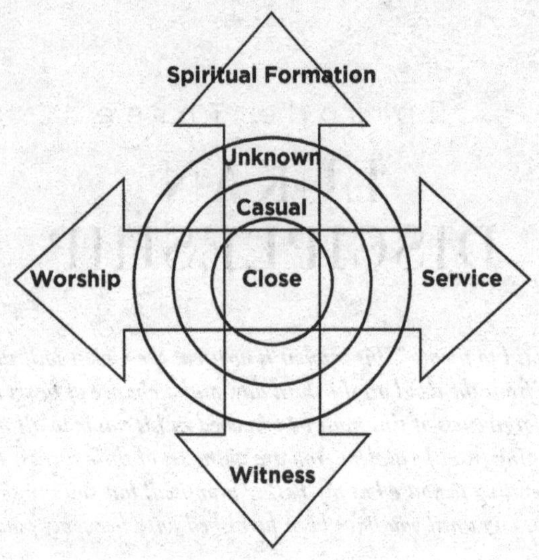


# Representative Characteristics from Luke's Gospel

### *The Lord Sent Them Out in Pairs*

Two by two. Luke and Acts is distinctive because those who carry the word and mission of Jesus tend to go out in pairs. Compare the sending out of disciples in Matthew. In Matthew, Jesus sends out the Twelve, and they are presumably sent out alone, or at least we are not told that they travel together (Matt 10). In Luke, though, not only are Seventy-Two disciples sent out, we are specifically told they are to travel in pairs (Luke 10:1). It is also notable that the Seventy-Two are given instructions related to hospitality (e.g., how they enter a house, whether they are greeted well in that house, how they are to be a guest in that house, Luke 10:5-9), and once they have been received, they can go to work healing; in Matthew, Jesus tells his disciples where to go (to the lost sheep of Israel) and what to do when they get there (heal, cleanse, expel demons, Matt 10:5-8). Luke's Gospel, just prior to the final instruction about a changed heart, closes with a pair of disciples on the road to Emmaus who are then joined and changed by Jesus as they walk (Luke 24:13-35).

Acts continues this pattern of traveling in pairs. While there are some exceptions, such as Philip's encounter with the Ethiopian eunuch (Acts 8), the characters tend to strike out on missionary journeys in pairs. Paul travels with Barnabas at first. When they have their falling out in Acts 15:36-41, it is over traveling companions, which leads to them going separate ways but still with a companion (Paul with Silas and Barnabas with John Mark). Even someone with as strong an ego as Paul chooses to travel with others. There was safety in numbers, but this partnership pattern is well established in Lukan faith communities.

So it is also true today. Lukan disciples prefer to walk with others on their faith journey. In fact, solitary acts of faith simply don't feel as fulfilling for Lukans. Definitely when they step out in evangelistic activity, they want others with them. They also want to know a household well before they introduce the life-changing relationship with Jesus into the mix. Luke and Acts are relational books, and they give rise to relational disciples.

## *Hearing the Backstory*

We hear significant stories about Jesus's conception, birth, infancy, and childhood in Luke's Gospel. These stories only appear in Luke's Gospel. We learn here that John the Baptist and Jesus are cousins, since Mary goes to stay with Elizabeth while they are both pregnant. We learn of Joseph's extended family as they go to Bethlehem for the required census. We are treated to the story of the holy family going up to the Temple, where they are welcomed and recognized by Simeon and Anna. Finally, Luke is the only one who gives us the story of Jesus ditching his parents to go teach in Jerusalem, and while he certainly asserts his authority to teach, we are also told that after they have found him and he has a teenager moment, he returned to Nazareth and was obedient to them (Luke 2:51). This backstory helps us relate to Jesus and his shared life in a family.

Family is experienced differently in Luke than in Matthew and Mark. In addition to more background on Jesus's extended family, we see him later interact with that family a little differently. When Jesus's mother and brothers show up to see him after he began his ministry (recall that in Mark they show up because they think he is out of his mind, Mark 3:21), in Matthew and Mark Jesus names the disciples gathered around the table before him as his brothers and mother (Mark 3:33-35; Matt 12:48-50). Meanwhile, in Luke, Jesus does not specifically designate others as his mother and brothers, but rather says that those who hear the word of God and do it are his mother and brothers (Luke 8:19-21). In Luke, conceivably his mother and brothers are within earshot of his words and can still be included in the family. In both Matthew and Luke, Jesus admits he has come to divide families. In Luke, however, there is an expression of the anguish that Jesus is experiencing as that reality comes to be (Luke 12:49-53), while it is a matter-of-fact announcement in Matthew (10:34-39), which is accompanied by the expectation of action: picking up a cross and following Jesus.

So family is a more positive experience in the life of Jesus in Luke, relative to Matthew and Mark. Family can include those who are close biological relatives as well as others who believe in Jesus like we do. Lukan disciples, then, tend to think in terms of family when they join a community of faith. Lukans will talk about church in terms of family. They may call their pastor brother or sister. Family implies strong, nearly unbreakable ties. Lukans depend on that kind of relationship with the people who share their faith journey.

### *Table Fellowship*

The kitchen table is one of the most important places in the house when a family gets together. In Luke and Acts, gathering around the table is central to who they are. It is how they bring all the people together. It is also how they more clearly see Jesus. Remember the travelers to Emmaus at the end of Luke? It is when they break the bread that they suddenly see Jesus who has been in their midst all along.

Whereas in the Lukan witness people gather around the table to see Jesus, it is also important that everyone be included. This means eliminating or mending whatever divisions are before us. Peter receives a table-based vision in which he is commanded to eat of things that are unclean (which violate the dietary instructions). He is then given the opportunity to go to the house of a Gentile, Cornelius, and is able to baptize Cornelius in the faith. Peter can sit at the table of Gentiles, and Gentiles can join the table of the faithful (Acts 10).

Another aspect of inclusion at the table is revealed when we compare the parable of the great banquet in Luke 14:16-24 and in Matthew 22:1-14. Both tellings reflect outrage at the people who refused the invitation. In Matthew, however, the host responds by telling his servants to go grab anyone they can find, whether evil or good. When someone comes to the dinner wearing the wrong clothes, however, that person is bound and cast out where there is weeping and grinding of teeth. Ultimately, the lesson in Matthew teaches that "many people are invited, but few people are chosen" (Matt 22:14). This dinner party is about who will be excluded. While the story told in Luke does acknowledge that those who refused the invitation will not be welcome, when there is space at the table, the host specifically tells his servants to "go quickly to the city's streets, the busy ones and the side streets, and bring the poor, crippled, blind, and lame," and then when there is still room, to "go to the highways and back alleys and urge people to come in so that my house will be filled" (Luke 14:21, 23). No one except those who refused are excluded. In fact, deliberately people are invited who would not normally be invited to such a thing and who presumably do *not* have the right clothes to wear.

Lukan disciples are committed to open-table fellowship. Such disciples defend open communion in the churches in which they worship. They also will be insistent that everyone should be welcome in God's house. It does not matter what you wear. It does not matter what abilities you have or lack. It does not matter if you are in the majority or the minority. It does not matter who you are, though they will want to get to know who you are. Whoever you are, you are welcome. Whoever you are, you will be loved.

### *The Least, the Last, and the Lost*

Whoever you are, you will be welcomed. And if you are particularly vulnerable, you will be sought, and not just to come to a fancy dinner. Luke is full of stories unique to the Gospels that tell about a savior who will do anything to reach anyone. A few of these unique characters include the widow from Nain and her son (7:11-17), the woman who is bent over (13:10-17), the shrewd manager (16:1-12), the rich man and Lazarus (16:19-31), the ten persons with skin diseases (17:11-19), and Zacchaeus (19:1-10). These characters are vulnerable in some way, or are addressing someone else's vulnerability, and Jesus makes space for each.

At the heart of Luke's Gospel are the three parables about loss: the lost sheep, the lost coin, and the lost sons (Luke 15). Extravagant grace is at work in these three stories, when the shepherd leaves the ninety-nine to go after the one, the woman throws a party that probably cost her more than her coin to celebrate finding the coin, and the father welcomes home the son who squandered his inheritance and also goes out to invite the other stubborn son to the party. These stories model a faith that seeks everyone, a faith that goes after everyone.

And then there is the parable of the Good Samaritan, in which a traveler risks his own safety and expends his own resources to care for one who might otherwise be his enemy (10:29-37). This story is told to show who our neighbor is and how to love a stranger. Lukans are the disciples who try to fully live into this call. Lukan disciples really try to love God and love neighbor as fully as they can, and they often do so by welcoming the least, the last, and the lost. Lukans don't want to turn anyone away, even as they in actuality struggle to love as fully as they want to. But at least they want to.

## Typical Characteristics of a Lukan

People who need people: they're the Luk-iest people in the world. Followers of Jesus, who fit the Lukan discipleship type, focus their journey around the relationships they build and maintain. They are defined by the Greatest Commandment: love God and love people. They struggle sometimes to continue in this love for more and more people. It becomes so safe and easy to love ourselves. But if Lukans lean into who they are really called to be, they can love the whole world. Let's look at who Lukans are so they can claim that special identity.

### *People Are the Mission*

At first it seems tempting to say that Lukans focus on people over the mission. However it is more accurate to say that people *are* the mission. Lukans are less concerned with building a new house for a family than they are concerned with the idea that everyone feels at home, no matter where they are or what circumstances they find themselves in. When a Lukan makes a decision, the primary concern is not how much money it will cost or how much time it will take, but how people will feel about it. Lukans are driven from a space that values and protects the people they love and want to see all the time. They want to live fully into the Greatest Commandment. They want to love God and love their neighbor, as fully as they possibly can.

### *Potluck People*

Lukans show up for fellowship time. If you are a Lukan, you live for the church potluck! You also may be one of the people who knows how to spread the food out just right, and who makes sure that the centerpieces are on the table. Lukans flock to the spaces where people gather and share life together, and they aim to make those spaces as hospitable as possible. Lukans will grow restless if they don't have the time or space to gather with their folks.

One of the churches who tested this gospel discipleship model was strongly Lukan. They did not have time between worship and Sunday school; one led directly into the next. So without official direction, people simply started showing up thirty minutes before church, and they stayed thirty minutes after. You can try to restrict Lukans from their fellowship time (not that you should want to), but you will not be successful for long.

### *Can't We All Just Get Along?*

Lukans want to love all people. They will be the first to admit that loving everyone is hard work. The hardest ones for Lukans to love are the people they see sowing conflict or division among them. It is worth a Lukan's time to understand if those people are operating from a different discipleship type; in some cases there may be a misunderstanding of how others live into their discipleship preference. Lukans will do almost anything to avoid conflict. This means that Lukans will work toward peace, if necessary at expense of the mission, because shared love with the people is the primary goal. As a result, Lukans don't tend to take risks. Risks can upset people. Instead, they think, *Let's keep everything going along the way it has always gone, and then there will be no need for conflict.* This is also why Lukans, friendly as they are, are hesitant to bring anyone new or culturally different into their space. New people might raise questions that upset someone. Better to just not run that risk.

### *Naught Changeth Thee*

The lack of risk taking is indicative of this next trait, which is that Lukans are notoriously slow to accept change. Change is a fearful space for them. Why? Because too often when things change, people leave. So, if we never change anything, no one will leave. Change is inevitable, and at times so rapid that it disrupts nearly everything. The life cycles cause change. People move to get new jobs. Children are born. People pass away. Life does not stand still. Even if Lukans can on some level accept that reality, what they might miss is the fact that not everyone is a Lukan. Markans leave because they get bored and are tired of being in a place where people won't listen to the movement of the Spirit. Mattheans leave when the community quits doing anything, which happens as people age and can't be as active. Johannines leave because the pastor said something they don't agree with. The only people who don't leave are Lukans. So it is a bit funny that Lukans are so worried about everyone leaving, when it practically takes dynamite to get Lukans to leave. Lukans could take more risks and actually might then keep *more* people. They would keep the Lukans of course, but then also probably the Markans and the Mattheans. (Whether the Johannines stay is really more in the hands of the pastor.) So go ahead, Lukans! Take a chance and try a change. And remember those Lukan lines from the hymn quoted for this trait, "naught changeth thee," actually applies to your perception of God, and not to you.

### *We Need to Talk*

Still, let's be honest about how Lukans actually accomplish change. It's not ever going to be a quick process. Why? Because Lukans will want to make sure everyone who has a stake in a decision has a say in that decision. If the decision is a personal one, a Lukan will want to talk it over with everyone in their family who might be affected. This can range in stakes from what a family has for dinner that night to whether mom should take a new job. If it takes place at church, then that means that Lukans will want to talk to everyone in the congregation before a decision is made. Again, that can range from what will be served at the reception for the new pastor to whether the church should build a new sanctuary or not. It is helpful for Lukans to learn the difference between decisions with low stakes and high stakes. Yes, deciding something that will affect the faith journey of a congregation (such as instituting an intentional discipleship system) is probably worth churchwide conversations to get majority buy-in (you will never get everyone, and Lukans would do well to learn that too). But deciding who is going to work in the nursery next month is not going to deeply impact the spiritual health of most of the congregation, so someone can just make some calls and get folks lined up. Lukans love a conversation because it is a space where they can grow in relationship with others, but sometimes the conversation itself raises Lukan anxiety (because it is about a change—even a tiny one!) and a lot of heartache can be avoided by also avoiding the conversation altogether. Instead, spend the time catching up by the coffee maker and hearing stories of each other's children and grandchildren.

### *Lukan Spiritual Crisis: What Happened to My Small Group?*

During a denomination-wide conflict, one of the churches testing this Gospel discipleship model lost about twenty people. The majority of those people were in one Sunday school class and also were Johannines who left as a protest about errant beliefs. When the dust cleared, one person was left in the class. She kept identifying as part of that class for longer than one would expect. If you are Lukan, you probably understand. Lukans are very protective of their relationships. When their people leave, Lukans are deeply hurt. They are liable to be upset with themselves, with the pastor, with the denomination, even with God—anyone perceived to contribute to the loss of their people. A loss of their people is the one thing that can consistently move a Lukan to leave. Where will they go? Wherever their people went. The Lukans who stay will be the ones who have too many additional relationships in the church to go. If they have to choose between people they love who left and people they love who stayed, they will choose to stay. Much less change is involved in the decision to remain.

## Living Your Discipleship: Lukans

Lukans love to grow in relationships with people. Lukans also recognize, however, that relationships take time and attention. Lukans are often wonderful friends who invest the time needed to remain friends with people. What Lukans sometimes neglect to do, however, is pour as much attention into their friendship with Jesus as they do with the flesh and blood people around them. For this reason, it's important that Lukans make time for Christ like they make time for Christians.

The following few paragraphs will help Lukans recall their love for Jesus and make time in their lives for him. Each paragraph is filled with suggestions for such work, but you should feel free to let these suggestions inspire you to relate in ways that are meaningful for you.

## *Lukan Starting Point: Circle Up*

This chapter describes how Lukans move in concentric circles. Jesus's last words in Acts to the disciples make just such a picture: start here in Jerusalem in the first circle with the people you know best, move out to Judea and Samaria to the people within your reach, and then go to the ends of the earth to the strangers you don't know at all. Lukans can also conceive of each of these as wider and wider embraces of God's people.

To frame their discipleship, then, Lukans need to define their circles. That interior circle may be yourself. What do you personally need to do for you to grow in love for God? The next circle may be your worshipping community or small group. The next circle then would be your neighbors outside the church. Or you could make the first circle your family, then church, then community. Or you could take inspiration from the Greatest Commandment and define your circles in terms of love: love of God, love of self, love of neighbor.[1] However and wherever you start, develop a definition

1. That order feels a little weird because it is usually love of God, love of neighbor, love of self. However, to keep with the idea of moving out from closeness, we should seek to put God at the center of our lives, then recognize we need to care for ourselves in order to be ready to care for others.

of what each circle is. Of course, you can have more than three, but Lukans usually don't make this overly complicated. Lukans tend to be fiercely attentive to their relationships, so you don't want it to be too detailed and entangled. Also, no matter where you start your circle, make sure you have a circle that includes people you do not know well who are outside the church.

Once you have your circles defined, it's time to reflect on how you grow in each realm of Lukan discipleship. These spiritual realms are representative of typical realms of discipleship, but you are welcome to adapt them in ways that have meaning for you. Also, remember that you are working to grow here, so don't just fill in the circles with things you already do and share, but with things you need to start doing to grow closer to God.

*Realm of Discipleship: Spiritual Growth*

Spiritual growth typically involves personal practices or disciplines that help you stay in love with God. Many practices for Lukans can be done well in community, and need not be private or isolated. Some of these practices include prayer, Sabbath, fasting, and studying or praying scripture.

Pick one or two disciplines for spiritual growth. Then imagine how you can practice those in each of the three circles you have defined. Let's take prayer, for example. If you think in terms of home, then church, then neighbors, you can make a commitment to pray as a family every morning and evening. Then you may offer to lead prayer in your small group. Then you may make a commitment to go in early to your child's school and offer to pray with a teacher or someone in the front office. As you grow in your understanding and practice of prayer, you may try different prayer practices, such as making and sharing prayer beads, or doing a prayer walk in the neighborhood. With each spiritual growth piece that you are trying, keep pushing yourself to get out of your comfort zone, which is a real struggle for Lukans.

### *Realm of Discipleship: Worship*

Worship is a primary way to express our love of God. Being present and engaged is certainly one way to grow closer to God. However, Lukans need to make sure to keep traveling in their circles. So let's look at the circles of self, church, and neighbors. At a basic central level, bringing yourself to worship every chance you get is an important step, and if worship has not been a consistent part of your life, then you should start there. Then you move into contributing to worship in a faith community. So look for ways to start leading in worship.

And then, as you grow even deeper in discipleship, it will come time to take worship outside the church—with you leading that charge. Lukans can create warm worship spaces anywhere they go, if they are confident enough and have practiced enough with their own people. Lay speaking is another way to serve in this circle, which can result in helping to lead services in other churches or gatherings. In this realm, you may not make progress in all three circles at once; it's okay to gradually progress as you learn to love God more deeply.

### *Realm of Discipleship: Service*

Lukans are best at service on their home turf. So most Lukans will need to stretch themselves into the outer circle. Actually, that is the case with all these circles. For Lukans growing in love is easier with the people they know. Time to stretch!

So it is good to identify the ways you are serving in your inner circle. You might decide that one of your service disciplines will be to grab your family and go out and pick up litter together in the park, and then have a picnic. However, making space in their inner circle for someone or something new is a stretch discipline Lukans may actually need to take on. Is it time to retire the monthly pancake breakfast that is feeding insiders from the church? See if it is time for a new way of gathering and serving among you.

Then, Lukans need to be intentional about serving outside their boundary, rather than only providing services inside the church. When Lukans go out to serve, they should be attentive to the probability that they tend to talk only to each other. So as a Lukan, you might make your service commitment to go serve with another organization. You may even go alone, although let's be honest, you probably want at least one friend with you. So take one friend, but make a commitment with that friend not to talk to each other while serving, but instead promise you can go later to have coffee and talk about what you experienced together. Lukans need to practice the discipline of serving farther and farther out from the people they know, so that they get to know others. And the best thing about Lukans is that when they let go and make space for others, the kind of service they do can be actually transformative because they get to know the people they serve alongside.

*Realm of Discipleship: Witness*

Lukans need to use their two interior circles to practice their faith story. Lukans have deep faith. They just prefer that their faith experience does not interfere with their relationships.

Lukans tend to share their faith with someone whom they have a long-established relationship. Most likely, those two inner circles have people like that. So, a Lukan can make a commitment to practice sharing faith with those groups, so that the story is less intimidating for them and flows more readily. If the self is in your inner circle, cultivate the discipline of paying attention to how God is working in your life. Spend time each day reflecting on those moments. Then, in the next circle, agree to share one of those moments from time to time. If you have a small group, you may try opening such groups with all participants sharing where they have seen God at work that week. That helps reticent Lukans become more accustomed to talking about their faith.

Even if a Lukan gains ease in telling the story, it still does not overcome the obstacle of fear that sharing such a story too soon in a relationship will disrupt it. If that is still the case, then Lukans need to grow in the number of people with whom they have a relationship. So a Lukan goal concerning witness can simply be to get to know, and love, one new person. That goal, by the way, is really to love them, not to get them to church. Implicit in loving someone, though, would be a growing desire to connect that person to Jesus. That desire will naturally grow on a Lukan's heart. So then a Lukan will organically begin to share her faith with her friend, and begin inviting her to opportunities to meet God and God's people. Some people may think that Lukans are the most reluctant evangelists, because the way they do it is so slow. However, because they have deeply established a relationship with someone that then leads to integrating them into a relationship with God, Lukans may actually be the most effective, because they walk alongside others until others are firmly rooted in the faith.

# Your Plan for Living as a Lukan Disciple of Jesus

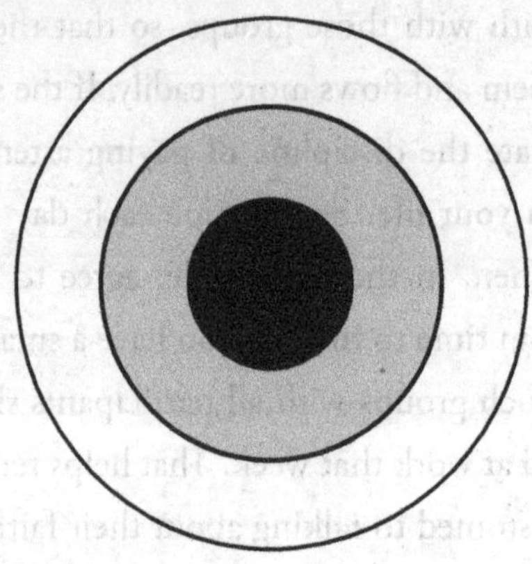

Identify your circles:

Circle 1 =

Circle 2 =

Circle 3 =

What will you do for each of the realms in each of the circles in the next year?

Spiritual Growth

Circle 1:

Circle 2:

Circle 3:

Worship

Circle 1:

Circle 2:

Circle 3:

## Serving

Circle 1:

Circle 2:

Circle 3:

Witness

Circle 1:

Circle 2:

Circle 3:

## Episode Four

# JOHANNINE DISCIPLESHIP

*When they finished eating, Jesus asked Simon Peter, "Simon son of John, do you love me more than these?"*

*Simon replied, "Yes, Lord, you know I love you."*

*Jesus said to him, "Feed my lambs." Jesus asked a second time, "Simon son of John, do you love me?"*

*Simon replied, "Yes, Lord, you know I love you."*

*Jesus said to him, "Take care of my sheep." He asked a third time, "Simon son of John, do you love me?"*

*Peter was sad that Jesus asked him a third time, "Do you love me?" He replied, "Lord, you know everything; you know I love you."*

*Jesus said to him, "Feed my sheep." . . .*

*After saying this, Jesus said to Peter, "Follow me." Peter turned around and saw the disciple whom Jesus loved following them. This was the one who had leaned against Jesus at the meal and asked him, "Lord, who is going to betray you?" When Peter saw this disciple, he said to Jesus, "Lord, what about him?" Jesus replied, "If I want him to remain until I come, what difference does that make to you? You must follow me." (John 21:15-17, 19b-22)*

In the beginning is the Word. That's how John's Gospel opens. Everything directs us toward learning from, listening to, being shaped by the Word. In the Greco-Roman world, Word represented wisdom. In John's Gospel, the Word is Jesus Christ. Yet Jesus is also the ultimate wisdom. Johannines seek access to that wisdom. They will gain access through mentoring by the Master. John's Gospel gives them a map for how and where that learning goes.

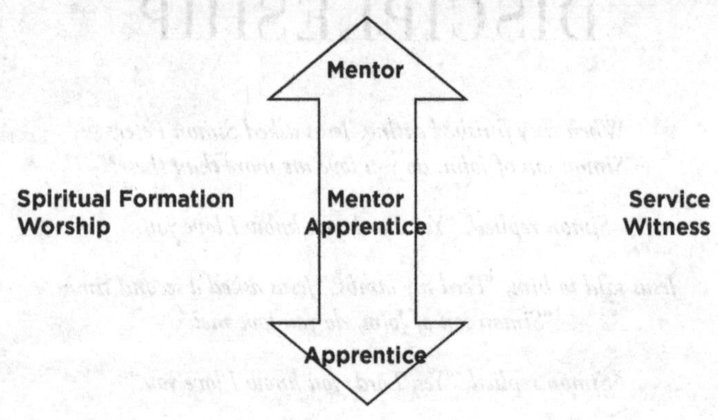


## Representative Characteristics from John's Gospel

### *So Many One-on-One Conversations*

John's Gospel is strikingly different from the other three Gospels. Matthew, Mark and Luke are called Synoptic (which means "seen together"), but 92 percent of John's Gospel is not found in the Synoptic Gospels. Many situations are different in John, and many characters appear only in John's Gospel.

A striking thing about John's characters is how much time Jesus spends in conversation with only them. In the Synoptic

Gospels, Jesus often interacts with the crowds. While he does encounter crowds in John, the vivid scenes of John are one-on-one moments.

We can start in John 3, where Jesus has an intimate conversation at night with the Jewish teacher Nicodemus. In this conversation we get "the gospel in miniature," John 3:16. But we also have one teacher instructing another teacher. Jesus is trying to mentor a very confused Nicodemus into seeing the new reality of God before him. This conversation is followed quickly by the conversation with the woman at the well in John 4. Jesus meets this woman where she is, engages her life situation, her theology, teaches her who he is, and then authorizes her to share that word with others. Even in "crowded" scenes, like the raising of Lazarus (John 11), Jesus is moving from one person to the next to engage them to broaden their understanding of what is possible in God's reign. He meets Martha first, and confronts her understanding of mortality by teaching his reality of resurrection. Then with Mary, he sees that she understands who he is through her worship, but also recognizes her emotions are overwhelming the space right now. Better to be present than to complicate things with teaching. Then he moves to Lazarus, and Jesus brings just what Lazarus needs—the words of life. Jesus's words literally transform Lazarus into a resurrected person.

Even Jesus's interaction with Pilate is more intimate. Jesus and Pilate pause and have a conversation that allows Pilate to ruminate on the definition of truth. This takes place in the shadow of an impending execution. It is an oddly reflective space between two men of inverted statuses (John 18:33-38).

The conversation between Jesus and Peter at the lakeshore is a continuation of a pattern established across the Gospel. Jesus will meet us one-on-one and take us to the next needed step to deepen our faith. Jesus also expects us not to stay in the same place as when we came to him but to have progressed in some way. He expects transformation. We do not always rise to that reality, but at least we have been invited into that place.

Johannine disciples, then, see these kinds of intimate exchanges as the ones that most likely result in growth because they can be tailored to the particular person and situation in which growth is needed. Yes, there is still a place for addressing the whole crowd, and important teaching can happen there, but for customized growth, face-to-face unique mentoring encounters are necessary.

### *The Beloved Disciple*

An intimacy in the relationships described in John's Gospel seems to be lacking in the other Gospels. This is the Gospel where Jesus strips down and washes the disciples' feet (John 13). Have you ever had your feet washed? It is an incredibly intimate experience. We are invited into Jesus's life in a more profound and private way in John than in the other Gospels.

Perhaps we see this most clearly in Jesus's relationship with the "beloved disciple." This disciple is never directly named, but he is present among the Twelve, and since this Gospel is traditionally believed to be written by John,[1] most readers assume the Beloved Disciple is John. References to the disciple Jesus loved commence in chapter 13 as the arrest and crucifixion of Jesus is imminent. The beloved disciple is reclining on Jesus's chest while they are

1. John 21:24 states that the one who wrote down these things is also that same beloved disciple Peter wondered about while he had his conversation at the lakeshore with Jesus.

at supper (13:23).[2] That moment is one of the most physically intimate moments in all the Gospels. There is obviously a deep closeness between them.

The Beloved Disciple is present at three additional scenes: at the crucifixion when Jesus makes his mother and the beloved disciple family (19:26-27); after Mary Magdalene announces the resurrection, he beats Peter to the tomb (20:2-5); and during the final fishing and lakeshore scene (John 21). These scenes occur toward the end of the Gospel, which could simply be a consequence of a developing relationship over time. The more time they spent together, the more the love and attachment has grown.

It's significant that one of the disciples is named in such a way. For followers shaped by John's Gospel, there may be a desire to be loved as much by Jesus as this beloved disciple is. Johannine disciples seek an intimate connection to Jesus. They will focus on following and loving the master teacher. They may also represent this desire by yearning to find a person in their life who best represents Jesus and then deepening in relationship with that friend or mentor. Johannines desire a closeness that comes from personal instruction from Jesus and those who teach about Jesus. They hope to be entrusted with Jesus's family and with the news that Jesus is risen because they have been invited into those personal spaces with Christ.

## *"I Am the Way..."*

Matthew contains the bulk of Jesus's teaching. John, however, contains unique teaching from Jesus. The teaching Jesus does in

2. The CEB translation states that this disciple was at Jesus's side (13:23) and then began "leaning back toward Jesus" (13:25). The Greek also supports "reclining on Jesus's chest" or "reclining next to him" (NRSV, NIV).

John is distinct because he spends the bulk of his time teaching about himself, while in Matthew Jesus tends to expound upon the law or teach about the kingdom of heaven. In John, though, we learn about who this Jesus is rather than what Jesus knows.

Jesus teaches about himself through the "I am" statements. These include the following:

- "I am the bread of life. Whoever comes to me will never go hungry, and whoever believes in me will never be thirsty." (6:35)
- "I am the light of the world. Whoever follows me won't walk in darkness but will have the light of life." (8:12)
- "I assure you that I am the gate of the sheep. All who came before me were thieves and outlaws, but the sheep didn't listen to them. I am the gate. Whoever enters through me will be saved. They will come in and go out and find pasture." (10:7-9)
- "I am the good shepherd. The good shepherd lays down his life for the sheep." (10:11)
- "I am the resurrection and the life. Whoever believes in me will live, even though they die." (11:25)
- "I am the way, the truth, and the life. No one comes to the Father except through me." (14:6)
- "I am the true vine, and my Father is the vineyard keeper." (15:1)

These seven statements help to define who Jesus is: provider, protector, revealer, the one through whom God and God's truth is revealed. Jesus, then, is the ultimate example for us to follow. Since he *is* the way, the path we follow as disciples is to listen fully to him and live as fully like him as we can. Johannine disciples look directly at the example of Jesus and let that guide their path. He is all they need for instruction. And his instruction comes to us through deep knowledge and study of his life through scripture, and through the lives of others who model him well.

*Love Each Other, but Others Not So Much*

The love expressed in John's Gospel is contained in a closed system. This is especially true when we look broadly at the Johannine witness to include John's letters. But even in the Gospel, there is a sharp distinction between those who are in the family of God and those who are not, starting from the prologue in chapter 1. The first chapter acknowledges the Word (i.e., Jesus) is light for everyone, but some will reject him, and those who reject him will not be in the family of God anymore, a family defined not by blood but instead by belief (1:9-14). Jesus's language is notably more personal in John when he calls his disciples friends, children, and brothers and sisters. But notice how such language is reserved primarily for his disciples, especially the more equal terms of endearment for friends and siblings. And when Jesus gives the new commandment in John, it is given only to those who were present just before he is arrested, and specifically it is given after Judas has left. Jesus says,

> I give you a new commandment: Love each other. Just as I have loved you, so you also must love each other. This is how everyone will know that you are my disciples, when you love each other. (13:34-35)

Notice that John's Jesus does not tell his disciples to love the unknown other. John's Jesus tells the disciples to love each other, and that love in this inner circle will reveal how they are following Jesus. Likewise, in 1 John 3, we are repeatedly reminded that we are known as Jesus's disciples because we love *our brothers and sisters.* Not everyone. If we hearken back to John 1, those who have rejected Jesus are not in the family of God. We do not have to love them. We just have to love each other.

Johannine discipleship that lives into a mentor-apprentice structure is subject to criticism because it looks like some are in the inner circle and some are not. Those who are select enough to be mentored by the significant leaders of the congregation, like the pastor, are viewed as privileged over the others. An answer to that objection is that usually those who are motivated enough to be mentored in a personal capacity, rather than getting enough from worship and any offered classes, are all being mentored, especially once the mentoring culture is firmly established. So if you are interested in being part of that circle, do the work to get there. But another response is that Johannines are living into the Johannine tradition. While the opening of John's Gospel reminds us that Jesus is open and available to everyone, not everyone will choose to believe and follow. Johannines will not feel much remorse for faithfully living the reality of discipleship as they understand it. If you want to be loved, if you want to be mentored, get in the game. No one is stopping you, though you may encounter belief requirements to get into the inner circle.

### *The Exalted One*

The closed system of love in John, which is lived out by Johannines in a mentor structure, could be described as hierarchical.

Jesus is set apart from us in John's Gospel; indeed, he is set above us as Lord. This distinction is made plainly evident in the predictions of Jesus's passion. Unlike the Synoptics, which tend to describe the crucifixion in tragic terms, John describes Jesus's crucifixion as his exaltation, as the author of John repeatedly uses the Greek word *hypsoo*, which means to be exalted or lifted up in these predictions (3:14-15; 8:28; and 12:31-33). Not only is the crucifixion a fulfillment of the will of God, it is the great moment of Jesus's lordship in John.

Johannine disciples do not see anything wrong with well-defined hierarchies, because hierarchies provide a clear stairway to reach Jesus Christ, the exalted One. Everyone is climbing a ladder to Christ. Ladders have structurally sound next steps. These hierarchies are not designed to be oppressive per se (though Johannines would do well to remember that oppression is a temptation here). They are meant to help people understand there is an orderly and narrow path for reaching Jesus, the head of us all. We will never be equal to him.

## Typical Characteristics of a Johannine

Johannines are the standard bearers of Christianity. If something suddenly happened to all the Bibles on the earth, we could turn to the Johannines and get it faithfully reproduced. They pay attention to the tradition, and in particular to Jesus as the great teacher and source of all wisdom. No wonder that the Gospel shaping them opens with a proclamation about the Word, which was also a synonym for wisdom in the Greco-Roman world. Johannines seek to grow in that wisdom, and that reforms many of their defining characteristics.

*At the Feet of the Master*

A Johannine would give practically anything for the chance to be one of the Twelve, to have the chance to travel with Jesus for personal instruction. In the absence of that experience, Johannines will seek to learn at the feet of people who do a beautiful job of living like Christ. For this reason, Johannines will seek a church in which the worship service centers around the sermon. They will also seek a pastor who serves as the kind of example they want to emulate. Johannines yearn to be mentored one-on-one by that kind of pastor. The most assertive of Johannines will actually ask for that to happen. Many of them will desire it, but they will lack the confidence to be so forward. However, Johannines should remember that not everyone can have that kind of attention from the pastor, and so they should be open to other mentoring possibilities as well. And they should aim to help someone else advance in their discipleship by serving as a mentor.

*(Almost) Sola Scriptura*

Johannines also tend to be our Bible scholars. They may be formal Bible scholars with a graduate degree or they may be informally trained. Many Johannines, such as the beloved and lifelong adult Bible study teacher, can go toe-to-toe in knowledge with anyone so trained. They are insatiable in their study of scripture. Because the Bible is the source of so much wisdom for them, they spend significant time with it. Therein lies the danger for Johannines. Perhaps more than any other type, Johannines sometimes cross the line from deep appreciation for the Bible to worship of it. The Bible may reveal indispensable beliefs about God, but it is not actually as holy as God. Since we talk about the word of

God (Bible) and the Word of God (Jesus), this does not help Johannines make that distinction either (especially since the phrase "Word of God" is crystallized in John's Gospel). Wise Johannines remind themselves often of the distinction between the person of Jesus and the words of the Bible.

### *Lifelong Learners*

Johannine disciples are never done learning. We've often seen frail saints dragging themselves down the hall on walkers and in wheelchairs to make sure they soak up biblical teaching in their Sunday school class every week. The disciples who do that to see the other people are Lukans; the saints who do that to hear good teaching are Johannines. Because they desperately want to learn, they will let you know if they can't hear the teaching or preaching. Johannines take extra classes on all kinds of things. They may have multiple educational degrees in multiple subjects. They book vacations with an explicit learning component. For instance, a Johannine might travel to France and Italy and seek cooking lessons with a renowned chef, once again learning at the feet of a master. Of course Johannines enjoy learning put to good use, but practical application often is incidental to them. The point is to learn. There is value in that whether or not such learning is applied or produces an income.

### *Great Expectations*

Johannines are the Christian standard bearers, and what high standards they have! Consider yourself special if you have the admiration of a few Johannines. Because Johannines value the example of great leaders so much, they have high expectations for those leaders. They know, theoretically, that leaders are still human, but they somehow expect them not to be. Johannines can forgive a misstep here or there, but repeated missteps or significant sins will not sit well with Johannines. Because they have these high standards, they are looking for potential faults, which means that Johannines can be highly critical of leadership. They may also be the greatest supporters of leadership in a ladder system, especially when they admire them or have a leader as a mentor.

Johannines will also have high standards for their church. They make less room for error at the table, whether those errors are behavioral or, honestly, from incompetent people. The irony here is that their commitment to high standards also makes them susceptible to taking on unacceptable behavior. While frustrated about how things are going in a faith community, Johannines can get rather insistent. In some contexts (particularly among Lukan disciples), they will get away with harping, and the next thing you know, they are the church bully. There is great power and usefulness in having people in our church who take their faith so seriously, and churches should value that. However, Johannines need to remember that there always must be room for other people, none of whom are perfect (including themselves). A welcoming space can allow for growth. Johannines really love growth. Focus on growth instead of conformity.

*Accused of the Humblebrag*

John's Gospel has a "mysterious" figure referred to as the beloved disciple. That disciple is not explicitly identified, but we all know who it is! Nearly everyone is sure the beloved disciple is the author of the Gospel. Humblebrag. Johannine disciples sometimes come off arrogant, and honestly, some of them are. They feel like they have put in enough work to claim a space for their wisdom. Some Johannines, though, are mistakenly perceived as arrogant when in actuality we are seeing an assertion of their high expectations, especially around a statement of faith or a creed. Johannines do well to remember that they are sometimes perceived as arrogant. Others who interact with Johannines, rather than writing them off as an irritating braggart, should take time to dig deeper beneath what they are saying, to discover the passion of their faith and learning.

### *Johannine Spiritual Crisis: The Mighty Have Fallen*

How often have we seen a great Christian leader fall? One of the results of such a fall is a spiritual crisis among all the Johannines who follow them. Johannines don't always readily extend trust to a leader. Like all of us, Johannines can be taken in by charismatic tyrants and narcissists, but the fallout is deeply traumatic for Johannines. When they do put trust there, they need it to hold. If the leader falls, a Johannine disciple will often question everything learned from that leader. This can extend to biblical lessons learned. Ultimately, this can rock a Johannine to the very core of faith and belief. To guard against such fallout, Johannines need to remind themselves who is actually worthy of worship. We do not worship a pastor. We do not worship a teacher. We do not worship a compilation of scripture. We worship the triune God who incarnated as Jesus Christ. Keep the main thing the main thing, and such a fall will be less damaging.

## Living Your Discipleship: Johannines

Johannines love being disciples. In fact, they would really love to be one of the Twelve, sitting with Jesus and learning directly from him. In the absence of that reality, however, they will instead seek to learn from those who have spent a significant piece of their lives learning from Jesus. Eventually Johannines grow into the people who do the teaching. For the average Johannine, however, that is an extended process. Since learning is how Johannines grow, we will look at that process in this section. The material above shows how Johannines understand themselves. The rest of this episode is the practiced faith for that understanding. Johannines have a very simple, yet deeply transformative way of growing in their faith. Intentionally practiced, then, their discipleship takes hold.

*Johannine Starting Point: Get a Mentor, Be a Mentor*

To repeat, Johannines love to gather at the feet of the Master. They really want that Master to be Jesus; in fact, the Master *is* Jesus. But since they don't have Jesus walking around with them, they grab the next best thing: someone who really does well at talking about and living like Jesus. Johannines are constantly looking for someone to help them imitate a life like Jesus, recognizing for sure that they themselves will never actually be Jesus—though a corrupt Johannine will start acting like it. Johannines, then, will have high expectations for anyone who mentors them. Because of these high expectations, Johannines may actually connect with more than one mentor, choosing particular people based on what a Johannine thinks she can learn from that person.

A young Johannine may start out with mentoring at a distance, such as listening to great sermons in church. But all Johannines should recognize that to truly grow in their discipleship, they need to develop a closer relationship with someone who can guide them. But not everyone can pick the pastor in a church with more than twenty adults! A pastor can mentor one or two dozen people (at most) effectively and deeply. So most Johannines will need to find someone else. This means that Johannines also need to serve as mentors. Despite their love of and commitment to the mentoring process, many Johannines struggle to leap over to becoming a mentor. Actually, it is probably because they so value that relationship that they are hesitant. Johannines often struggle to believe they have the knowledge and wisdom to guide someone meaningfully. A Greek professor in seminary observed our own hesitation to teach others Greek: *You only need to be one or two chapters ahead of your students to teach them something.* Not only are there several people Johannines can learn from, there are a great number they can teach. If anything, adult Johannines have years of life experience compared to youth. That is wisdom people need. You can pick among different mentors because each person has different realms of expertise. In the same way, you may be chosen as a mentor in a particular realm because of your specific wisdom in that space.

### *Realm of Discipleship: Spiritual Growth*

Johannines are typically most comfortable with the practice of studying scripture. It is fine to lean into that tendency. The challenge is to keep leaning. Johannines can get stuck in a rut in the ways they study scripture, because they have defined expectations about how growth is supposed to happen. Expectations are a good to have, but staying boxed in perpetuates the same knowledge (and potential misinterpretations) over and over and over. Memorization is not the same as transformation. In fact, it may work against it. So, if a Johannine is accustomed to learning about scripture by listening to the Sunday sermon, and then doing daily readings on her own, then it is time to change it up. You may want to join a Bible study or make the commitment for a deep communal walk through one book of the Bible. Or a Johannine may need to stretch himself and try some scriptural experiences like *lectio divina* or Ignatian imagination. Remember that this knowledge is not meant to be stored in yourself for your own edification. A maturing Johannine will also commit to teaching others about scripture too.

As appealing to Johannines as the discipline of studying scripture is, everyone needs to be well-rounded in their discipleship. So while you may lean into studying scripture, you need to stretch yourself. This means growing in practices like prayer, bodily disciplines like fasting, and participating more fully in Christian community. Sometimes Johannines can start behaving like lone wolves, focusing on individual growth. Johannines need to challenge themselves to be actively engaged in learning about God alongside others. Let that help frame how you need to grow as you make your discipleship plan.

### *Realm of Discipleship: Worship*

The only way worship services will be a struggle for Johannines is if they don't like the preaching or don't respect the preacher. The sermon and the chance to learn from an admired teacher drives Johannines in the door. However, their standards are high. Johannines are the ones who will both deeply appreciate a great sermon and let you know when they didn't like it. So, for Johannines to grow in worship, there are usually two things they need to do: understand and appreciate the other elements of a worship service, and start to train as a worship leader themselves.

The understanding and appreciation of worship for Johannines is a matter of education. If a Johannine can be mentored in the value of the other aspects of worship, and taught to see how and why all those elements tie together, it will increase a Johannine's capacity for learning in that space. It also means that Johannines can then become significant servants in ministry teams such as a worship committee. Once they understand the purpose and theology behind the whole, they can be great advocates for and passionate developers of powerful worship.

Then, as a Johannine matures and gains confidence, Johannines need to develop their own capacity to lead worship. This practice may start at home. Then they might help with youth worship, serving as mentors for the youth who are leading. Or perhaps they lead worship as a ministry team is out doing mission work. Johannines are slow to come into this role because their expectations are so high, but if they can be carefully nurtured in it, they will likely fully come into their own as channels for scriptural Christianity.

### *Realm of Discipleship: Service*

Johannines are significant servants—when they know they are good at something. Before they have confidence, they are reluctant to step out. In fact, sometimes they would be pushed to do even the things that they are good at because their own personal expectations are so high. In some small groups that include couples, a partner might have the opposite gifts than their partner. For example, one partner loves working for a mission organization in her church, but she would never have done it if her spouse hadn't pushed her into it (the spouse knew she would love it). The one who pushed her out the door was Markan/Lukan; the one who had to be pushed was Matthean/Johannine (and she is one of the Mattheans in the video). The Matthean in her loved to serve, but the Johannine in her wasn't sure she could do it.

So perhaps a Johannine needs to take stock of her gifts. What are her areas of expertise? Where does she shine? Once that inventory is taken, the next step is to ask, "How can I better use these gifts for the benefit of the Lord's kingdom?" Johannines can also take stock of things they are interested in but could use more skills. Then the next step is to figure out who could mentor them in that type of service. Those two steps allow a Johannine to both share their gifts as a mentor and to be mentored in gifts that are rising. And remember, serving does include typical Johannine gifts like teaching. It is not necessarily about picking up a hammer and building a wheelchair ramp.

*Realm of Discipleship: Witness*

Well, sharing the faith might be the hardest space for Johannines. It is not that they think it unimportant. Johannines passionately desire that everyone know about God, particularly by affirming knowledge or beliefs about God. Sometimes Johannines think this knowledge so important that only professionals should do it. However, Johannines may need to build up a great deal of courage (they would say "expertise") around this practice before they can share the good news with others outside their system. On the other hand, once they have that courage, Johannines may be a little overzealous if not pushy in their approach.

Critical to growth in witness for Johannines, then, is education about our post-Christendom context. Johannines can be very effective evangelists. They may need to understand that we can't stand on street corners and yell at people to repent and expect to make one bit of difference anymore. Helping Johannines understand our twenty-first-century realities can help them grow in this space. So, Johannines, you may want to be mentored by a Lukan in this space, someone who can teach you the value of relationship building. Or you may want to investigate technology-based expressions of your faith. What would it look like for a mature Johannine to begin a blog or podcast where she shares her faith with others? A thoughtful, social media teaching space could be a great outlet for a Johannine. In whatever way Johannines learn to share the knowledge (and love) of God, they need to be empowered to share the gospel of Christ with others.

## Your Plan for Living as a Johannine Disciple of God

What do you need next to advance in spiritual growth? Who could mentor you in that space?

What do you need next to advance in worship? Who could mentor you in that space?

What do you need next to advance in serving? Who could mentor you in that space?

What do you need next to advance in witness? Who could mentor you in that space?

In what realm of discipleship do you feel you could mentor someone?

Who or how could you begin (or continue) to mentor?

# QUESTIONS

In the course of testing *Gospel Discipleship*, frequently asked questions emerged about this process. For additional support, visit www.gospeldiscipleship.net.

## Born to This Type, or Formed by This Type?

As the tally of discipleship types made its way in from his church, James, who is in the Markan section of the video, shared the results with me. Something about them was remarkable. We noticed a strikingly high number of Markans, especially for a United Methodist church. The interesting correlation is that James is the sole pastor tested who drew only from one primary discipleship type: he is almost entirely Markan. So James should lean more intentionally into his Markan discipleship practices, as there seems to be a significant contingent of people who are coming from a similar perspective.

The fact that his congregation, which he has served for almost four years, is leaning in the direction of his discipleship gifts, prompts us to wonder: Is a congregation gradually converted into the pastor's way of discipleship? Further data will illuminate this possibility, especially after a pastoral change. While waiting for more data, an educated guess is that nature and nurture are in a complex dynamic. We are born with all kinds of personality tendencies that are inherent to our created person. There is every reason to think that some of us would be born with a natural inclination toward action, some toward creativity, some toward building close relationships, and some who love to teach and be taught.

If I can use myself as an example, my secondary gift is Johannine. When my brother was two years old, which would make me four at the time (and not yet in school), my mother tried to teach Mark how to count. She said, "Say one, Mark." My brother said, "One two three four five" in rapid succession, and then started crying. Later she caught me with my hands around his throat screaming, "Say fish! Say fish!" Mom realized my poor brother had been subjected to my earlier teaching techniques. I am now much more reasonable with my teaching techniques, but a tendency toward teaching seems to have been wired into my brain from birth. Whether I picked that up from my nurturing parents, or if I was wired that way, is too difficult to determine. It was such an early a part of me, though, that for practical purposes, this is the way I was born, to be Johannine once I learned about Jesus.

I was also nurtured to develop my creativity. Again, we have a chicken and the egg question. Was I naturally creative, so I was drawn to experiences that allowed me to express my creativity, or was I put in situations that required creativity that naturally developed it? My creative experiences are again too early to untangle that question, starting with the fact that my mother painted my playroom orange because she read that orange inspired creativity. I was also raised in a family that preached the idea that everyone has value. Everyone has a story. And everyone has gifts to share with the world. Markan.

So perhaps we have a genetic leaning into one type of discipleship pathway or another. Our worldview and our self-expression, however, are not solely dependent on genetics. In addition to the impact of trauma, we are also shaped by the stories we share. The stories that we tell and the stories that are told to us help shape us into the people we are. Stories convey culture, including traditions and beliefs, and we are definitely shaped by the culture in which we grow.

When it comes to the Bible, this shapes us in two directions. First, as the Bible comes to have meaning for us, it also authors us by changing our hearts and lives. That transformation is the power that comes from the "authority" of scripture. We give the Bible special status when we refer to it as a holy (or sanctifying) text, and we then authorize it (in community) to shape who we are. Biblical authority need not be understood as top-down, "The Bible says it, I believe it, that settles it." Biblical authority instead can be understood in terms of the central story that shapes who we are.

That central story, though, includes four distinct retellings of the defining narrative for the Christian faith. Why? Why not just combine all four Gospels and make them fit together, eliminating any inconsistencies between them? The authorities who pulled the Bible together certainly had that option. They did not choose to harmonize. Why? Because they recognized that different Christian communities resonate with different narratives of the story of Jesus, because each of the Gospels had been written for different communities in the first place. With four witnesses that tell mostly the same story, but a story that is different enough to appeal to different kinds of people, the gospel has the capacity to reshape the diverse humans that populate this earth. God created us to be different, and God wants each of us in relationship. Telling God's story in different ways allows God to invite many more people into that story.

We may then be shaped by the story we are first invited into. Doug, one of the pastors who took the test and is in the Johannine video, showed up as primarily Johannine, secondarily Matthean, which initially surprised him. But then he reflected on his own experience. He was raised in an evangelical context in a church that centered around the pastor. His early pastor was a strong teacher and preacher. That preacher also preached almost exclusively on Matthew's Gospel, or at least that is how he remembered it. Was this future leader drawn to a church that had Johannine-Matthean tendencies, or was he shaped by his formative experiences? Nature and nurture are entangled.

It is possible, perhaps even likely, that a person may alternate their discipleship type as the need arises and the context changes and their experience in the story grows. Especially between your primary and secondary gift, your order could flip flop, just as when you take a spiritual gifts test in different contexts, top gifts change order based on the needs of the community in you serve. Take the test again at another time. See if your story has evolved, and see if that leads you in a new way of following Christ.

## Wait, This Doesn't Sound Like Me at All!

While testing the survey, we heard phrases like, "Well, this sounds familiar," or "This has me pegged exactly." But sometimes a person looks over the list of characteristics suggested by the scored result and says, "Yeah, I don't think this is me at all." When that happens, created space, either in the course of the conversation, or in a follow-up conversation later, allows people to share what exactly feels wrong about the results. Several understandings can help get to a place where you can better live into your discipleship, even if that means disregarding the results of the test and choosing a different path for following Jesus.

In choosing a different path than the one suggested by the test, try to avoid choosing the path you think is the "right" way of being a follower of Jesus. Most individuals, groups, or entire churches will say, "This test is very hard! I didn't want to choose just one answer to each of the twenty questions!" This is due to the probability that most of us have both a primary and secondary discipleship type. However, another aspect at work here is the exclusive narrative about discipleship that we are sold by some leaders. Sometimes we are told there is only one way of following Jesus. This feeling can be particularly acute if you are a different type than the dominant type of the people in your group or church. You may think you need to change to match them. That can lead to frustration and an exit. You need to live as the unique disciple you are, and you have a critical role to play in a group that has a different understanding of discipleship. You will likely be the one who challenges your community to do new things or see new people, or you may even be able to more clearly see when they are making mistakes. Every church needs their minority types, or they get too comfortable in their own way of doing things and quit challenging themselves to grow. So, if you do feel like the results are a mismatch and want to try another pattern, especially after you have examined the following questions, just try doing it for the right reason: because you want to fully live into the disciple you are called to be.

So before you switch types, ask yourself these questions:

1. **Has your story changed?** One young man, as part of a small group who did this assessment, announced before he received a result that he is afraid he took the test at the wrong time in his life. He took it after he had worked a very hard, very long day of work. So, he said, any of the questions that had anything to do with activity or doing something, he rejected straight out. Unsurprisingly, he scored low as a Matthean. Instead, he came out strongly Johannine. However, even considering a bad day at work, the more we talked through the characteristics, the more he nodded about being Johannine. At the end of the night, he thought he might have picked a couple of Matthean answers if he took the test again, but he also felt very much more at home in his Johannine identity. Still, the conditions under which you take the test may have an influence on how you answer. And this assessment admits that it is shaped by the stories that shape us. If you go through a significant event in your life, or even if just a long amount of time has gone by since you examined your faith practices, it is probably worth revisiting.

2. **Why do you do what you do?** One church flat out argued that they are not Lukan but Matthean instead. They insist that they are busy all the time, constantly doing things. They shared why they are Matthean: Every month they have a pancake breakfast. They also do meals for the teachers and take them little goodies throughout the year. They also participate in, and to a large degree, organize the festivals for their town. All these examples are actions, that is true. But ask, "Why do you do those things?" As each person gradually shared answers that essentially

stated that they do them to show love for people, note that their actions may seem Matthean, but their motivations are Lukan. A good space to examine is how they do business at their church council meeting. Let's say they need to vote on whether they should pursue negotiations to allow the town's chamber of commerce to have office space at their church. If the church is led by Matthean disciples, that would have literally taken five minutes: the pastor would have laid out the process, and they would have voted. Instead, if they are Lukan, they might spent thirty minutes talking about needing to install a new door in that room where the chamber would be located, so the church would look more professional and have a more welcoming space, and how the exit lights on exterior doors would need to be fixed so the chamber employees would know how to leave if there was a fire, and where would be the optimal place in front of the church for the chamber's sign, and so on. These are questions of hospitality and relationship, and questions that don't really needed to be asked before negotiations are underway. Before you jump ship on your type, ask yourself why you are doing what you are doing. Motivation may reveal your true type.

3. **Are there distinctions in how you live and grow and what kind of church you look for?** Because the assessment asks both questions about your own personal growth and questions about your ideal church, occasionally we see some results that reveal that someone personally grows in their discipleship one way, but seeks a church that lives discipleship out in a different way. For instance, one woman tested primarily Lukan and secondarily Johannine, who said she thought she is more Johannine than Lukan. A close look at her answer to particular questions showed she is self-aware. She clearly is drawn

> to the kind of study that Johannines engage in. However, she expects her church to lead first in love. So, if you agree that your top two types are reflective of you, but may need to be flipped, then try considering the difference in what you look for in church, and how you choose personally to live your discipleship. And also relish the possibility that you are likely one of those people who is called to be a minority type in whatever church you join!

If you have asked those questions, and it still feels like a miss, then it very well could be. Read through all the descriptions and find what pathway works best for you. Or take the test again and see if next time feels more accurate. Regardless of the route you choose for following Jesus, we would like to hear from you and learn about your experience. Visit the support website for this book, www.gospeldiscipleship.net. You will also find blogs there that update what we have learned since the book went to publication. It may prove helpful in discerning your path forward too.

Thank you for your interest in following Christ in the way God calls you. May your path be clear and satisfying as you draw nearer to Jesus through the Spirit.